Children Among Us

Photography by

LEO TOUCHET

Photographs of children from around the world

Children Among Us

Photography by Leo Touchet

Design: Leo Touchet

Type: Garamond

ISBN-13: 978-1-7324433-1-0

First Edition
July 2019

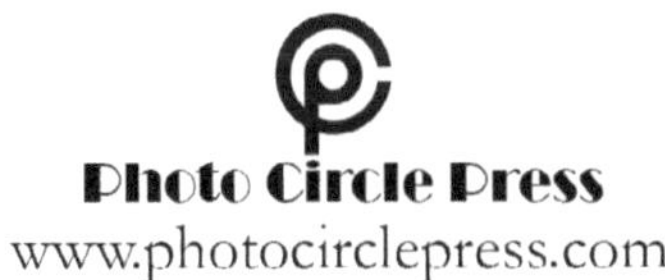

Photo Circle Press
www.photocirclepress.com

For the Children Among Us

In 2017, I had an exhibition of photographs of people from some of the many places I have been. The exhibition P*EOPLE AMONG US* was displayed in one of the galleries at the Acadiana Center for the Arts in Lafayette, Louisiana. The photographs in the gallery were all large 20 x 30 prints.

At the time as my exhibit opened in the gallery, there was a children's art night in another part of the Acadiana Center. Many families who were in the center for their children's art show brought their children to see my photographs.

The large photos in black & white photographs enabled viewers to see much more than they would normally see in smaller images. Of particular interest to me were the reactions of the children who kept pointing out details in the photographs to their parents who were standing nearby also viewing the photographs. Although I've had many gallery openings in the past, my experiences that night allowed me to see something new. Unlike adults who normally view art displays quietly, children get excited when they see something new.

Although a few photographs of children were included in the original exhibition, there were many more in my files which I have been cataloguing for over 10 years. This book contains 30 photographs of children from North America, Europe, Latin America, and Asia.

When I was six, my favorite uncle, Lucien Primeaux, returned home from the Pacific Theater in World War II with photographs from his during the war. I still remember those photographs and believe they were a major influence in my interest in photography. Hopefully this book will be seen by many children and will create a lifelong impression on them, as did the photographs which were shown to me seventy-four years ago.

Leo Touchet

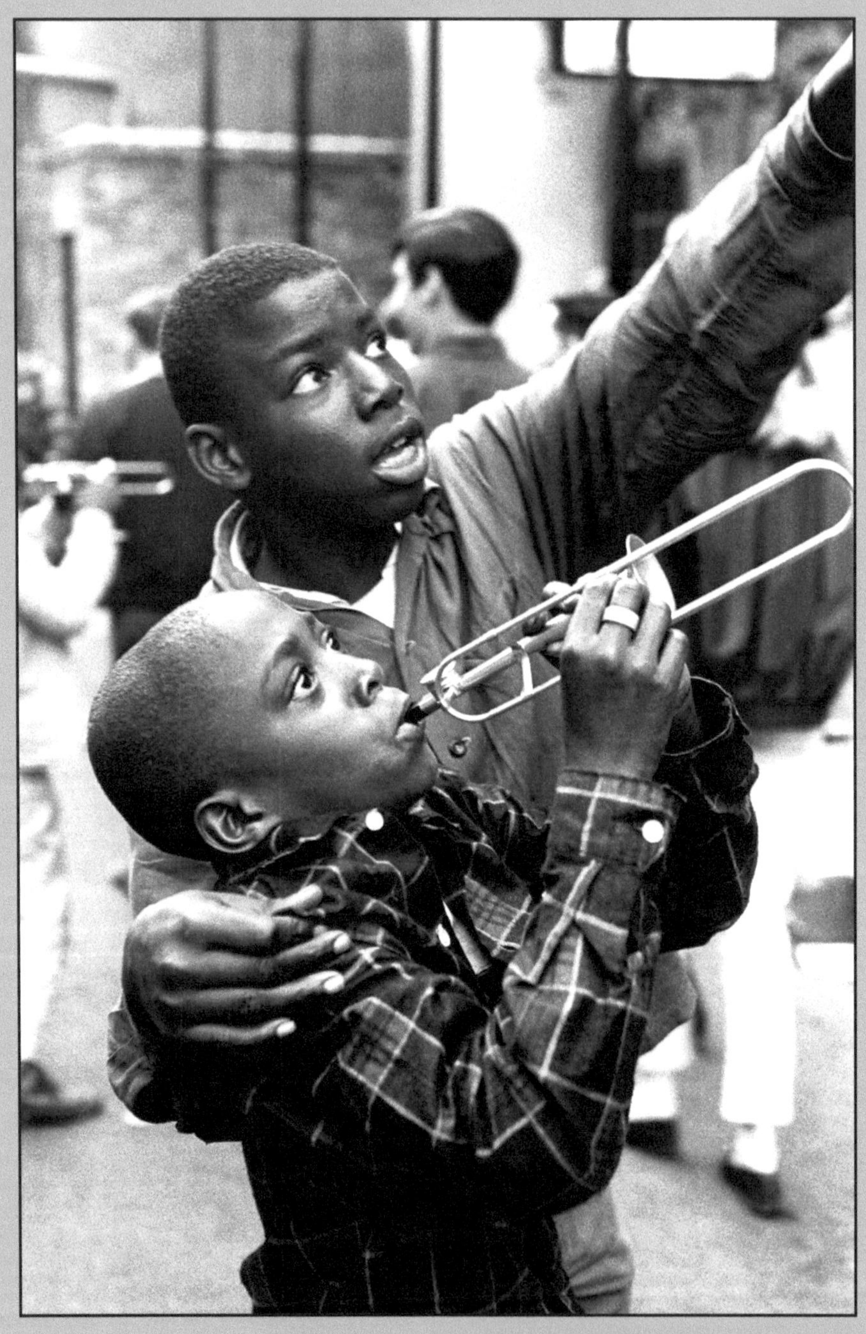

New Orleans, Louisiana - Bourbon Street in the French Quarter 1968

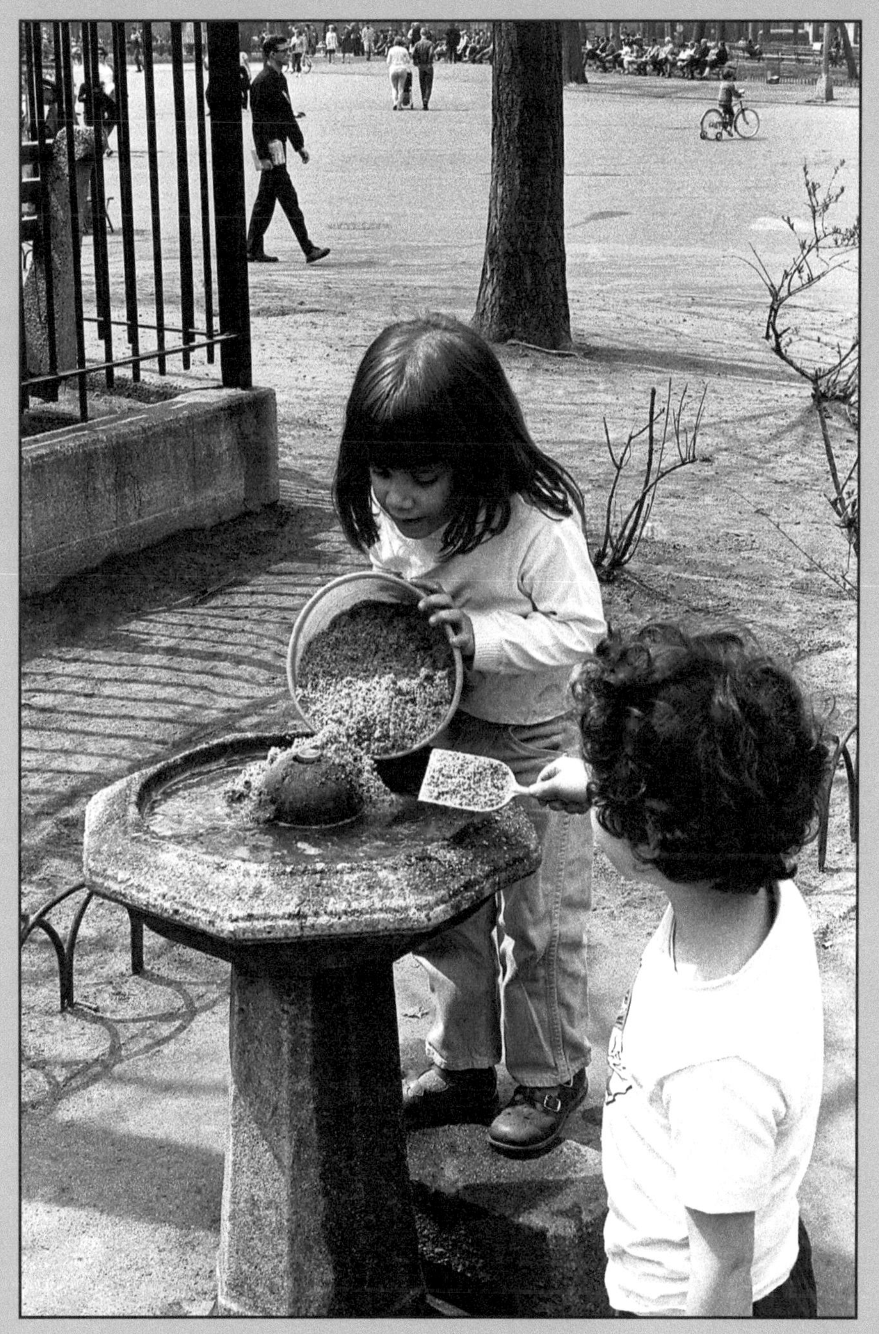

New York, New York - Spring Street in SOHO 1994

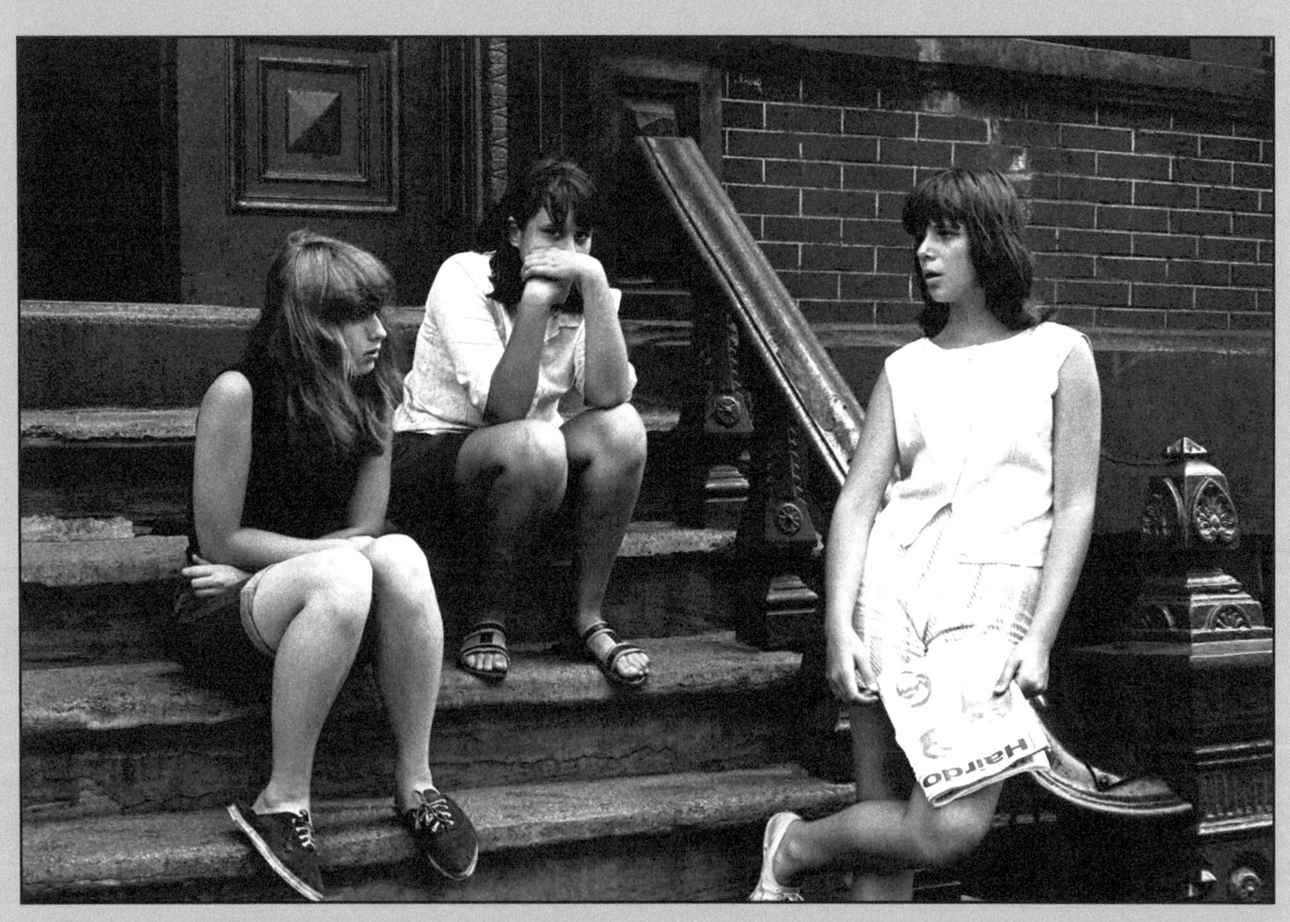

New York, New York - Lower East Side 1965

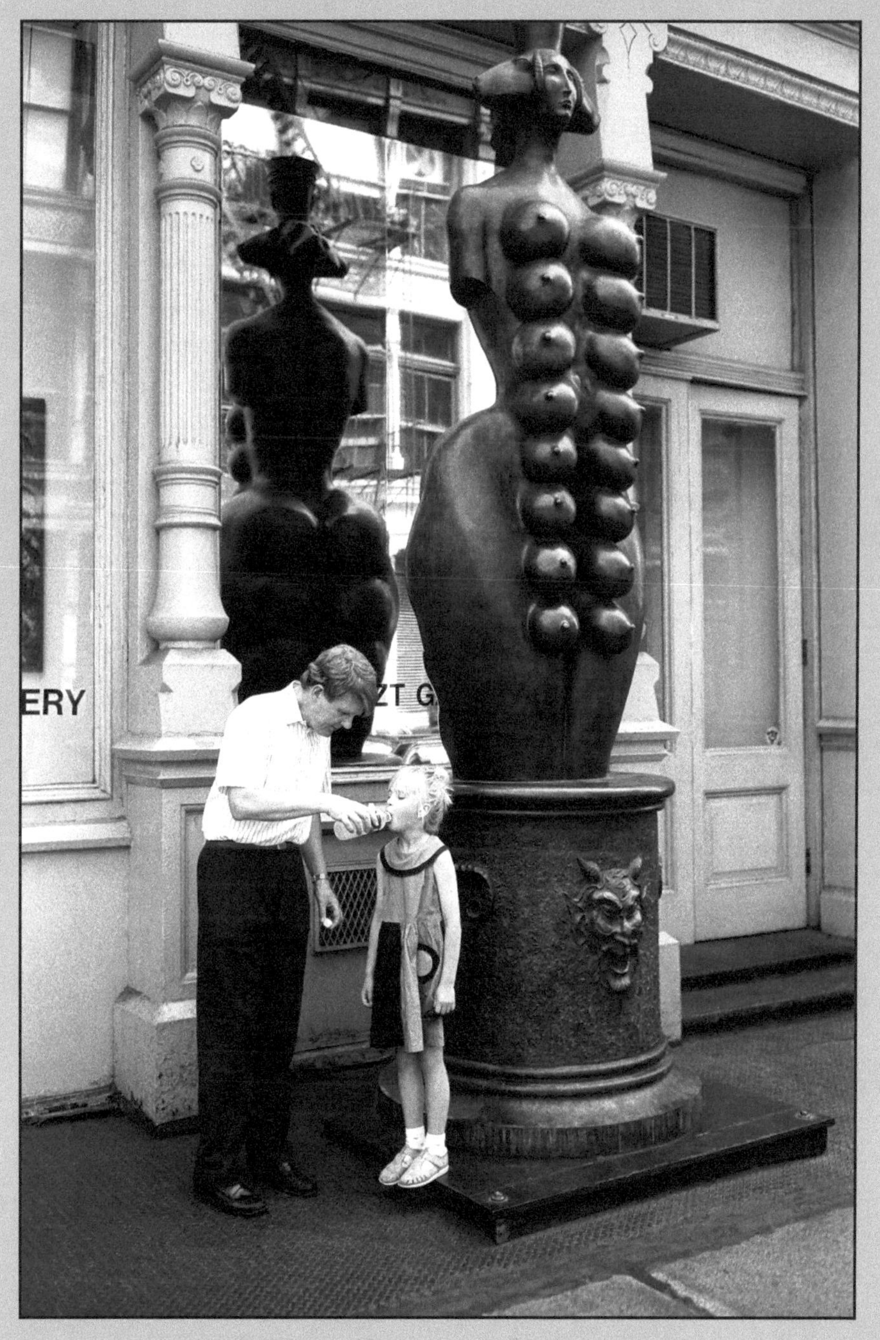

New York, New York - Spring Street in SOHO 1994

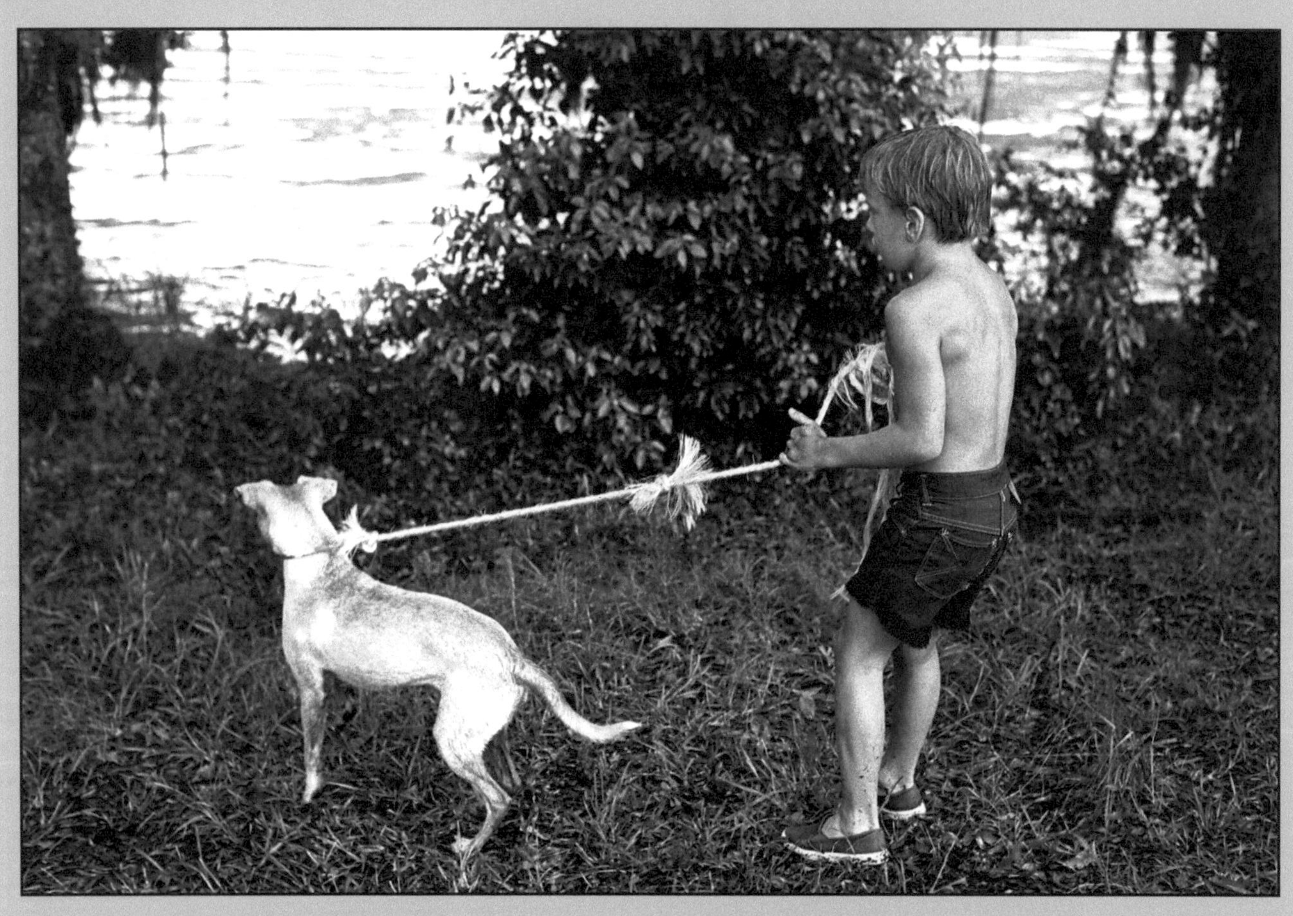

St. Martinsville, Louisiana - July 4th at Evangeline State Park 1973

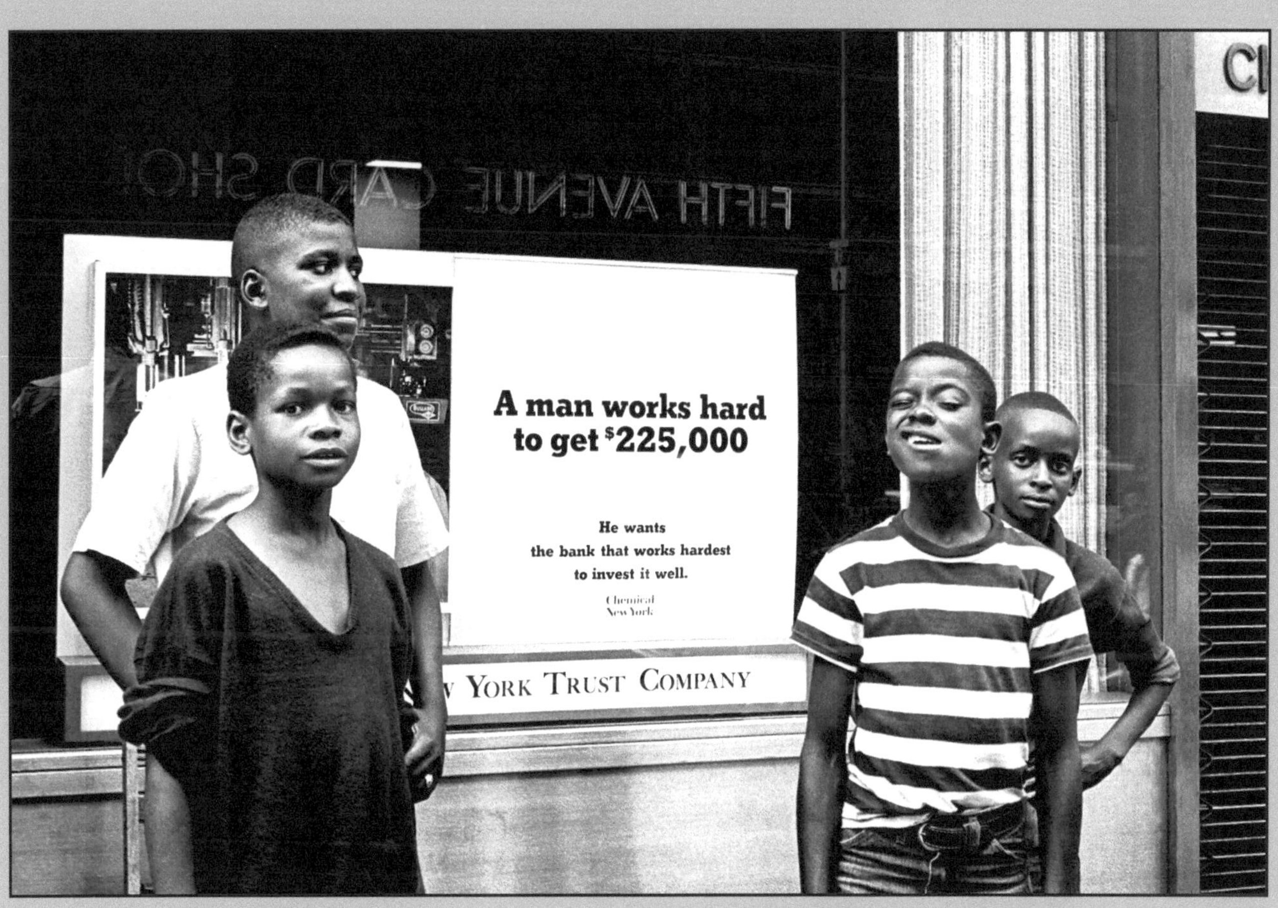

New York, New York - East 42nd Street 1965

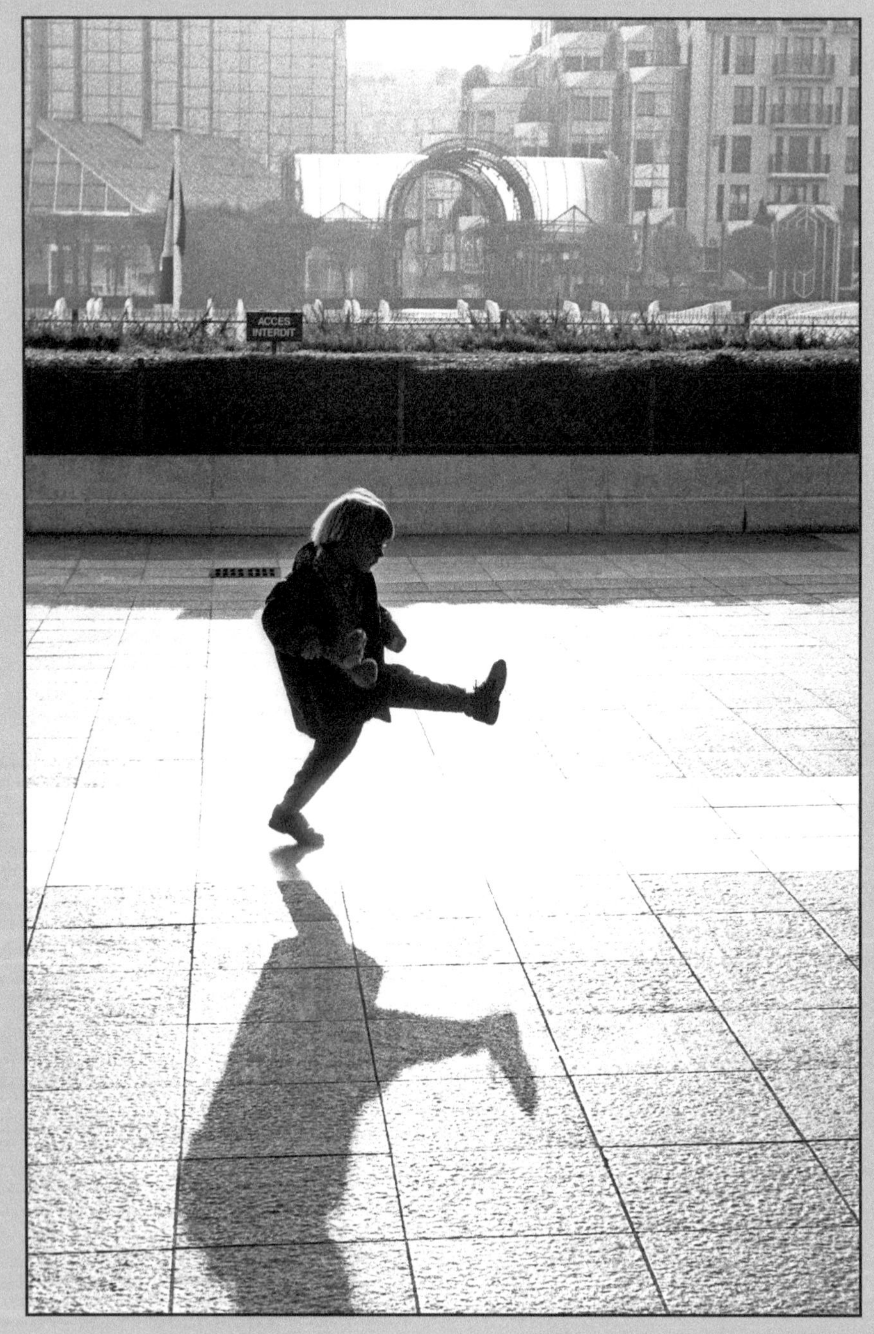

Paris, France - Forum Les Halles 1991

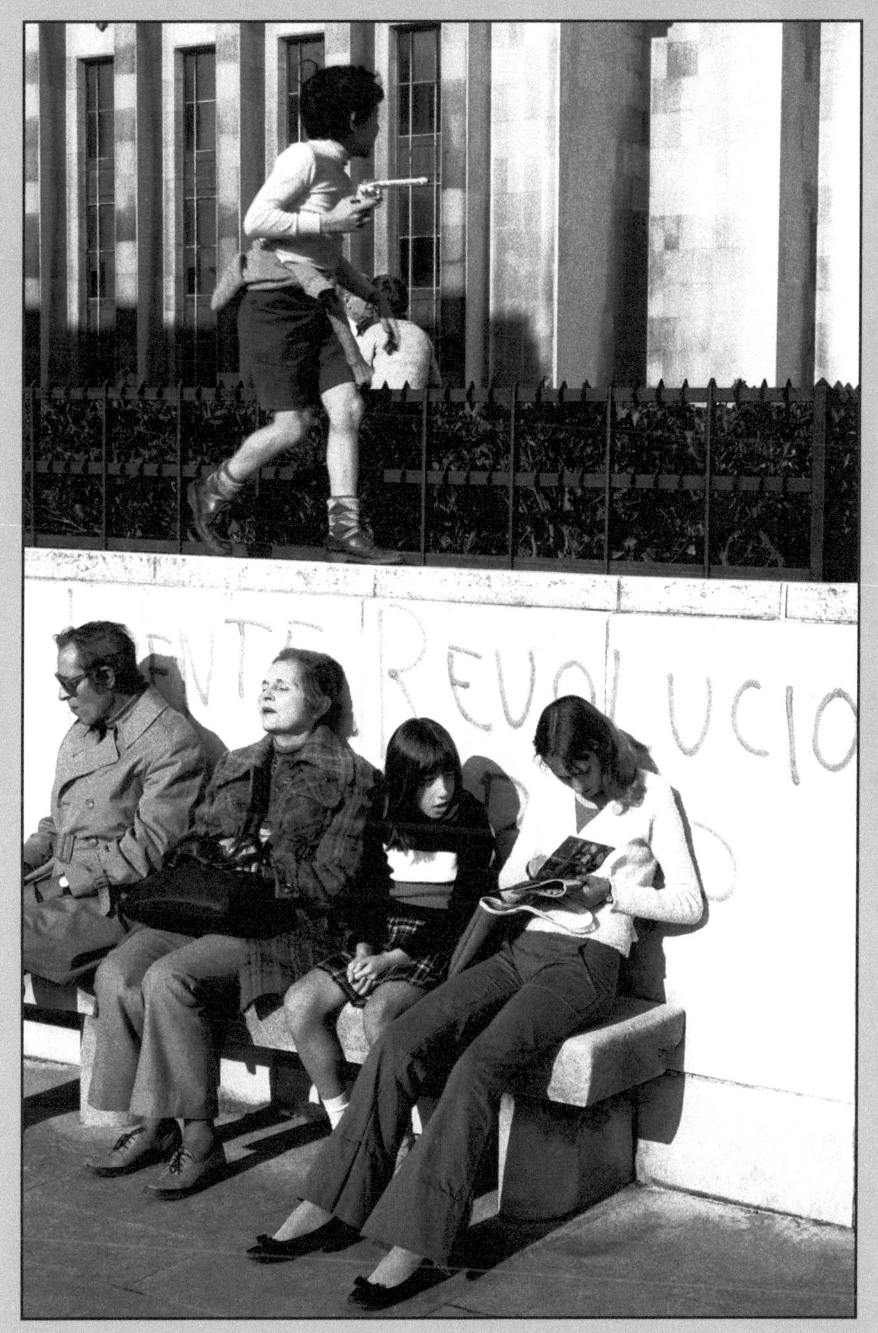

Paris, France - Trocadéro 1972

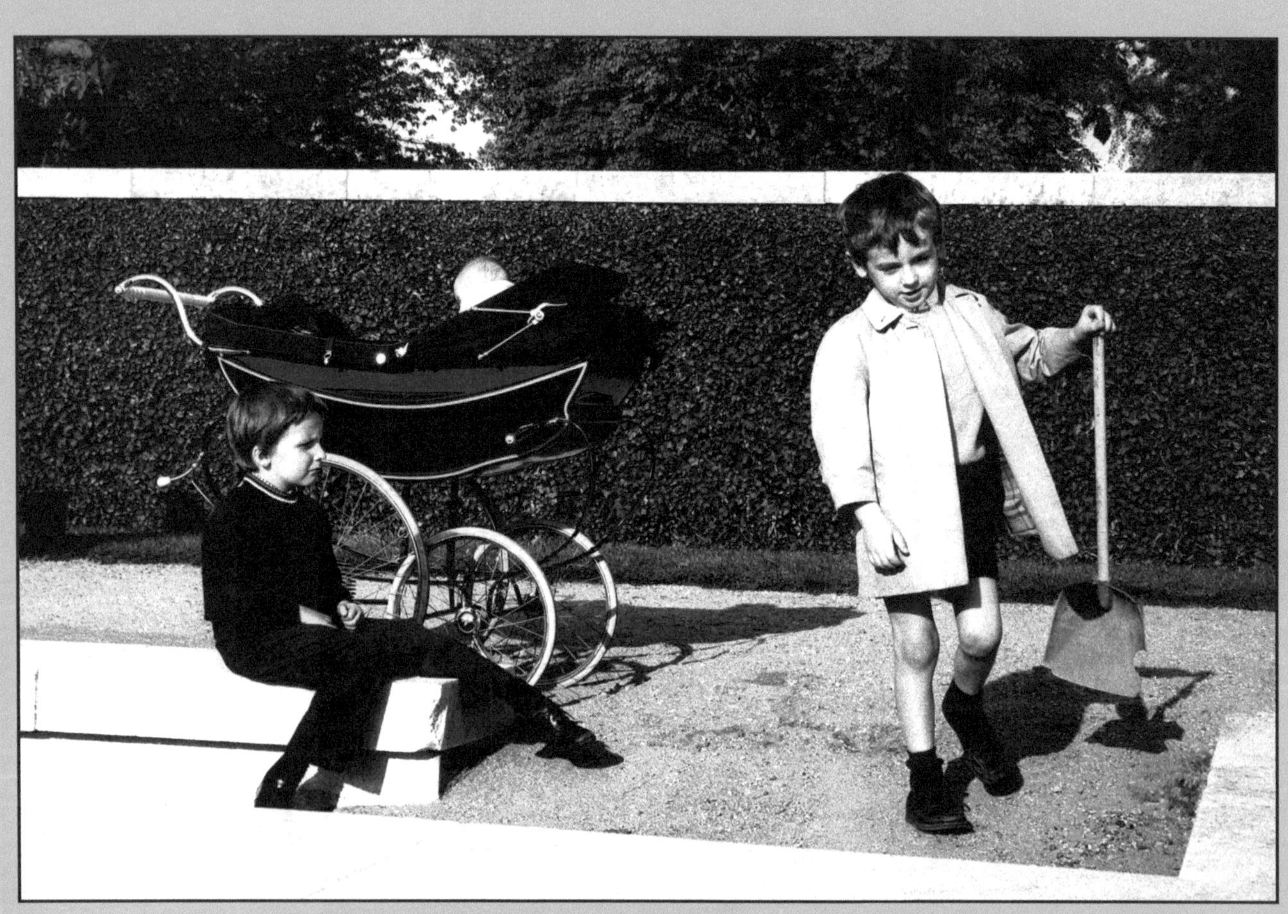

Paris, France - Trocadéro 1972

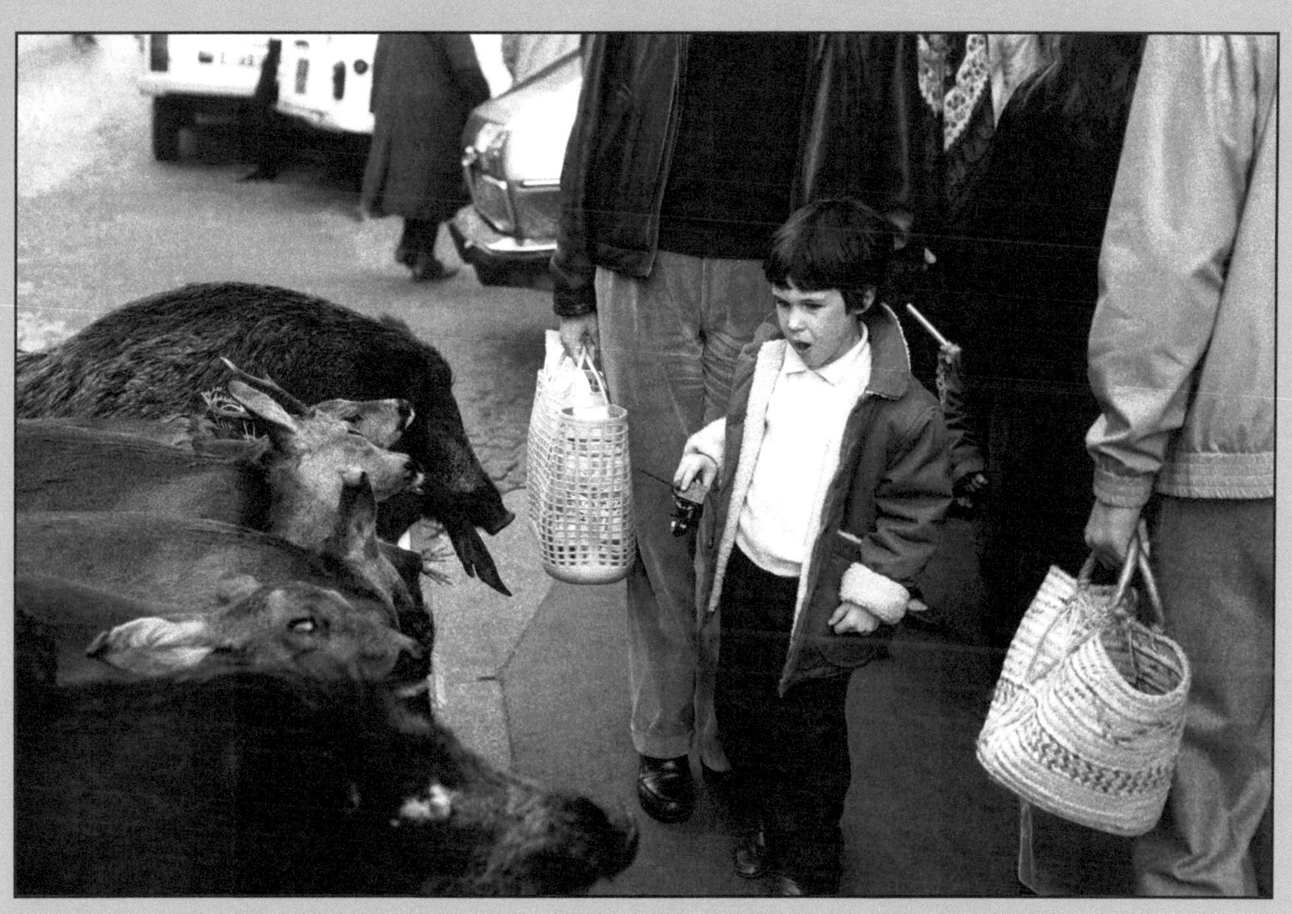

Paris, France - Rue Lepic Market 1984

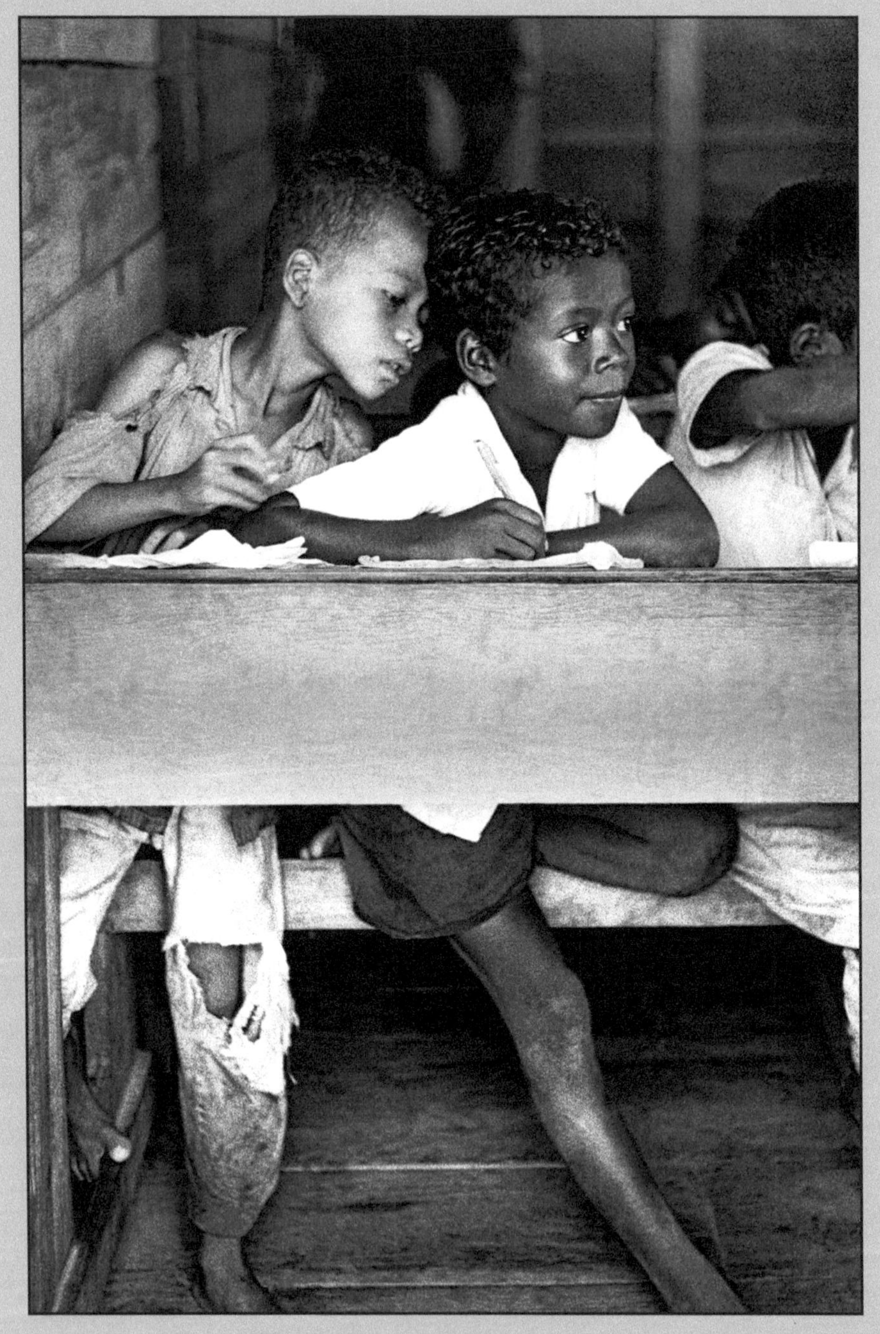

Puerto Lempira, Honduras - Miskito Indian boys in school 1968

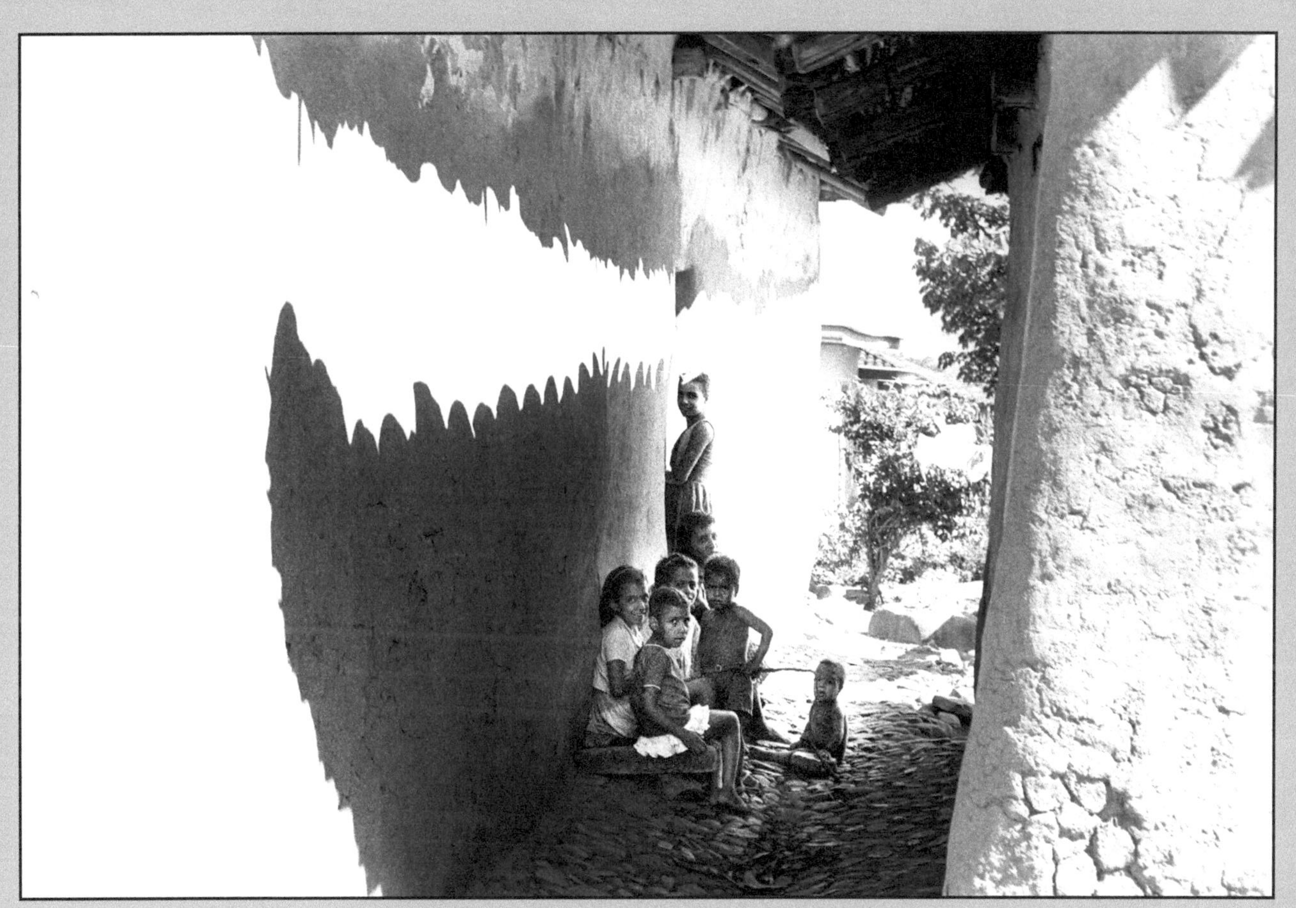

Yoro Department, Honduras - Coyoles 1968

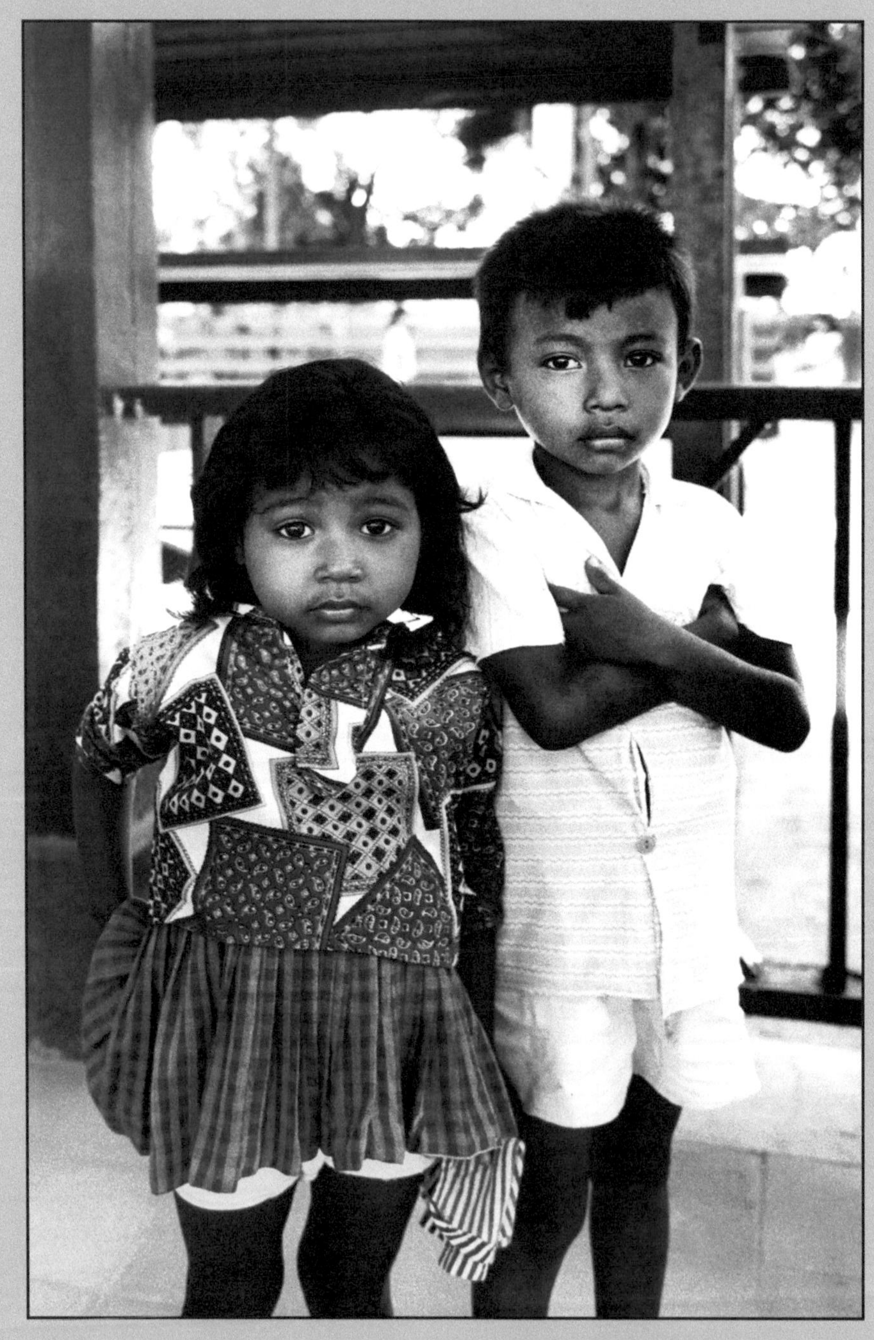

La Ceiba, Honduras 1968 – Brother and sister at school 1968

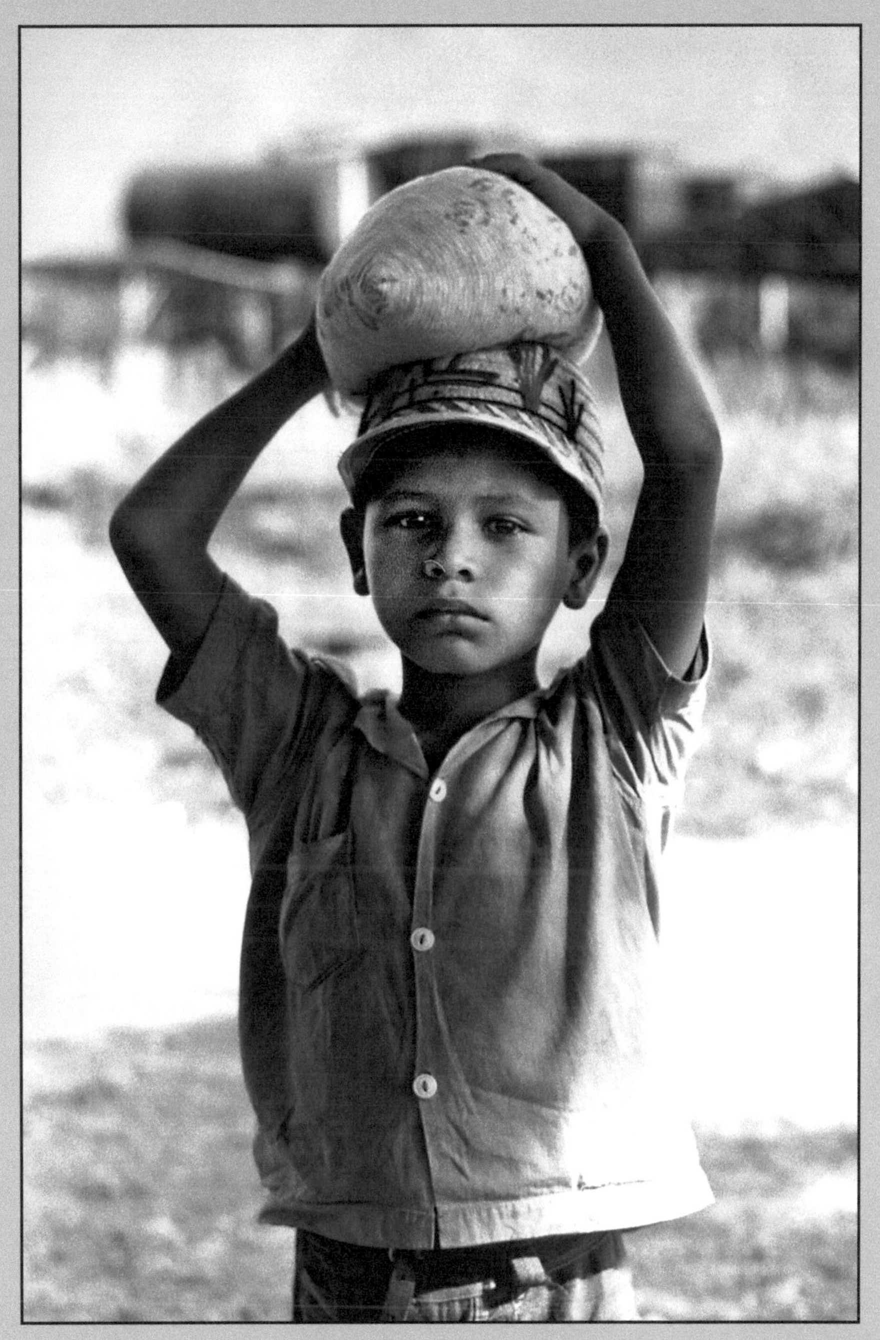

Yoro Department, Honduras - Coyoles 1968

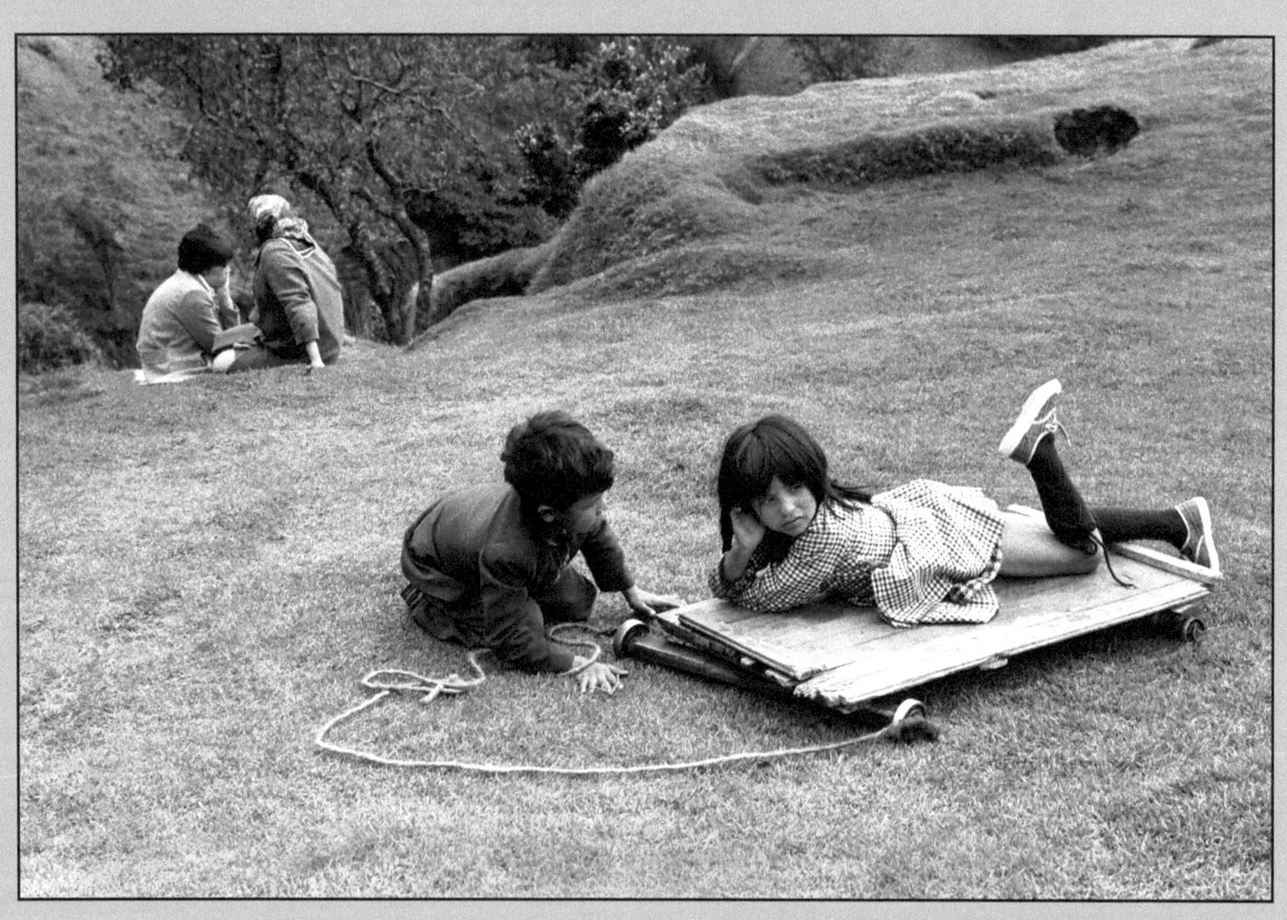

Tegucigalpa, Honduras - El Picacho Hill 1968

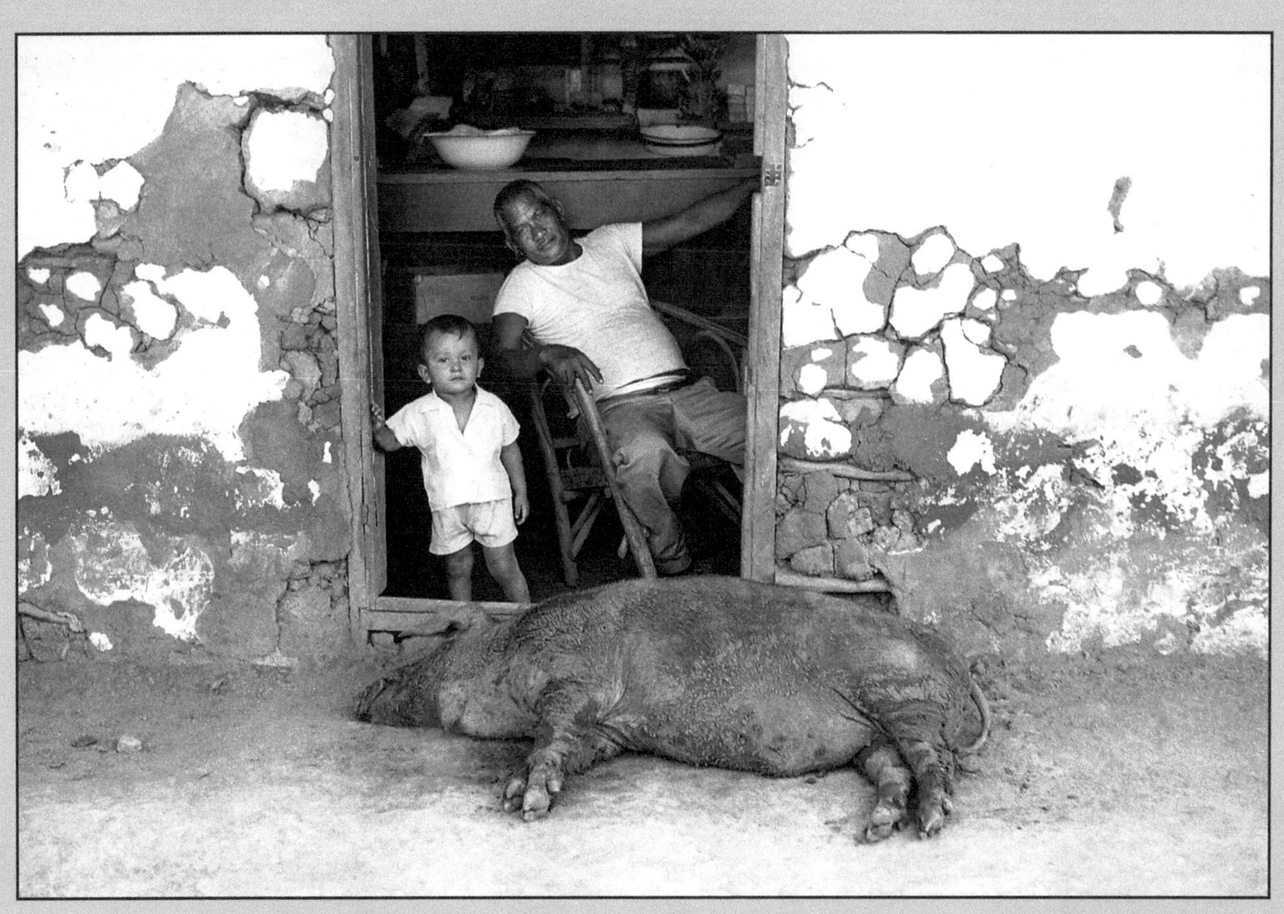

Yoro Department, Honduras - Coyoles 1968

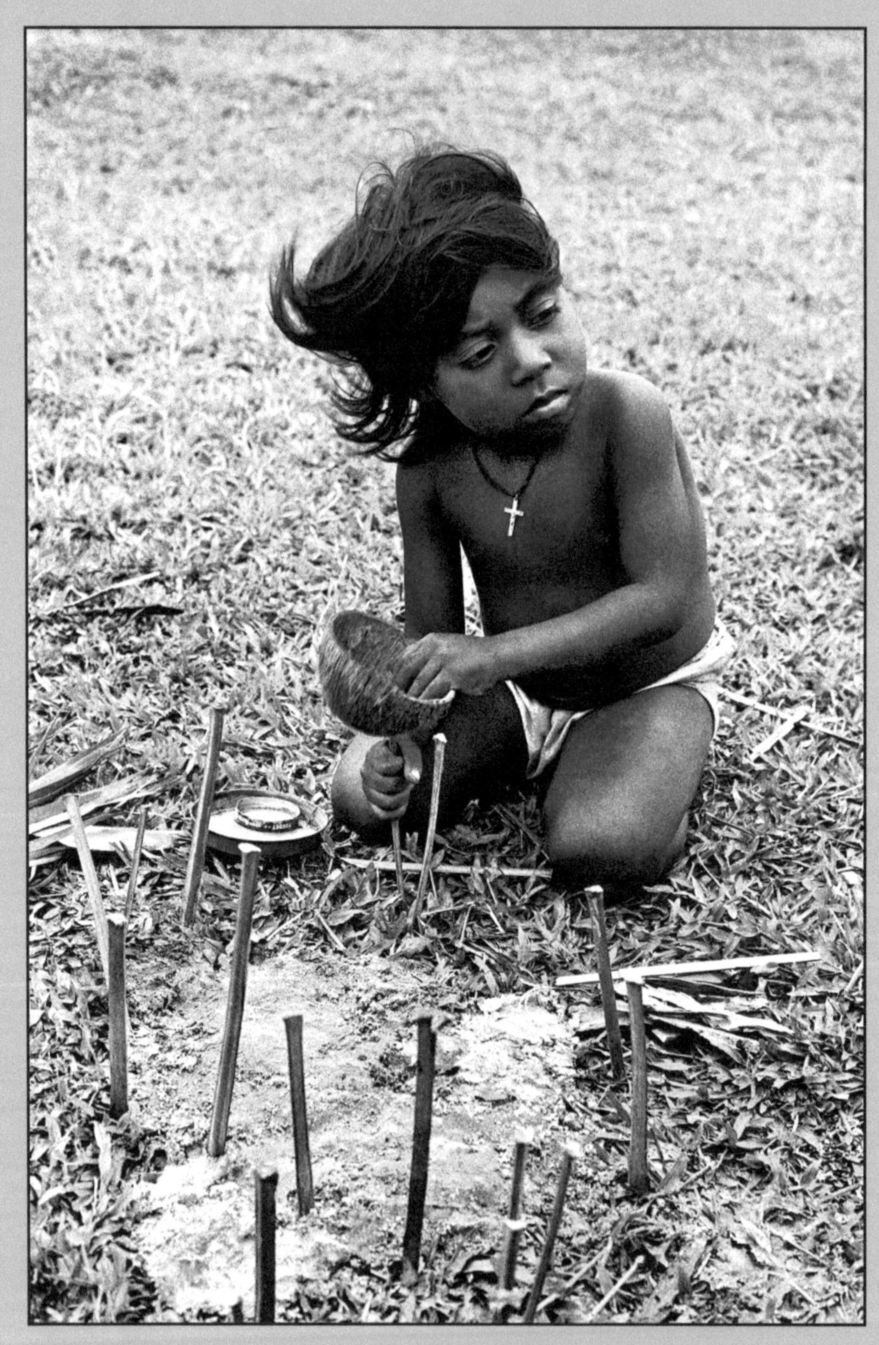

Puerto Lempira, Honduras – Miskito Indian girl 1968

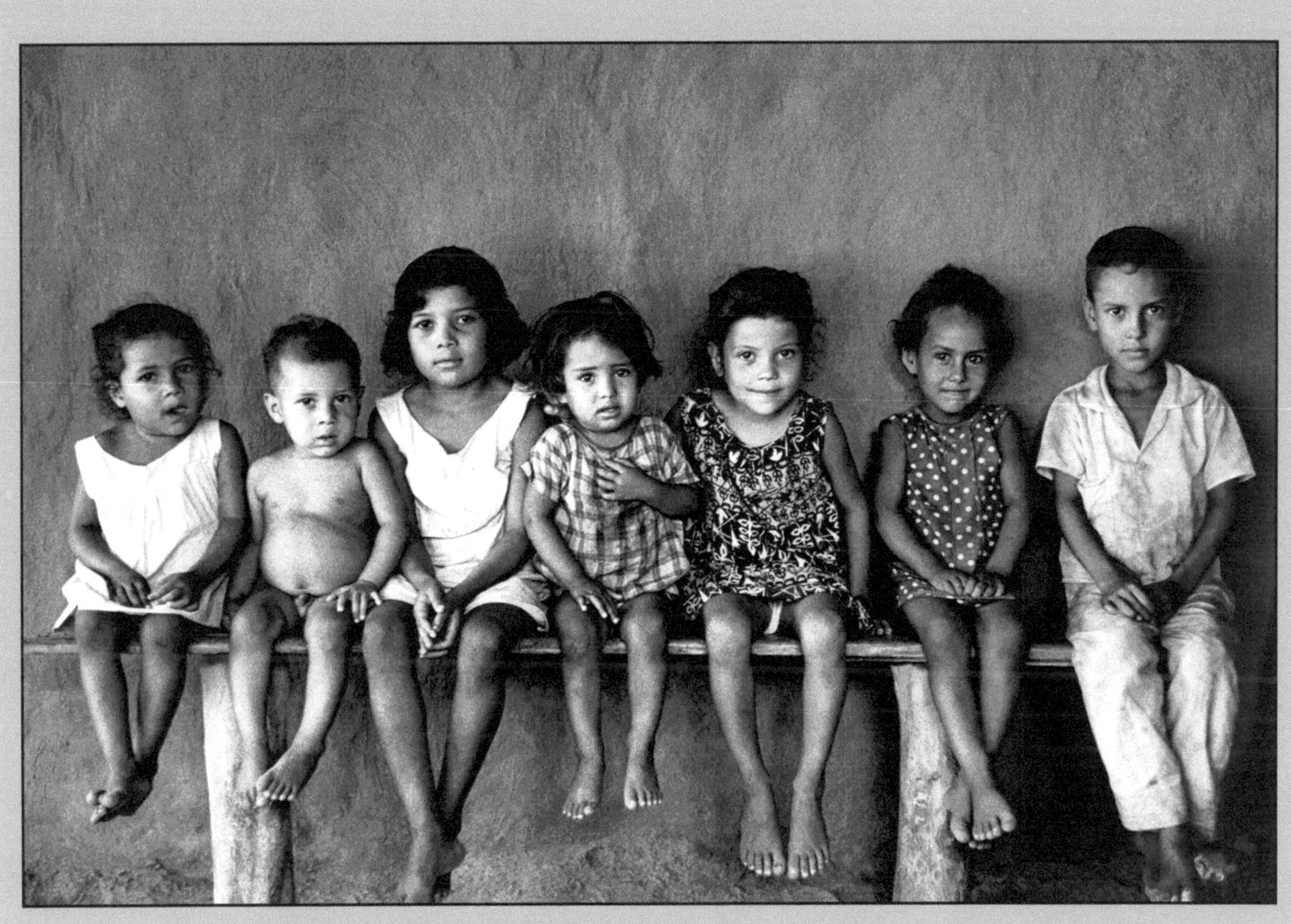

Yoro Department, Honduras – Coyoles 1968

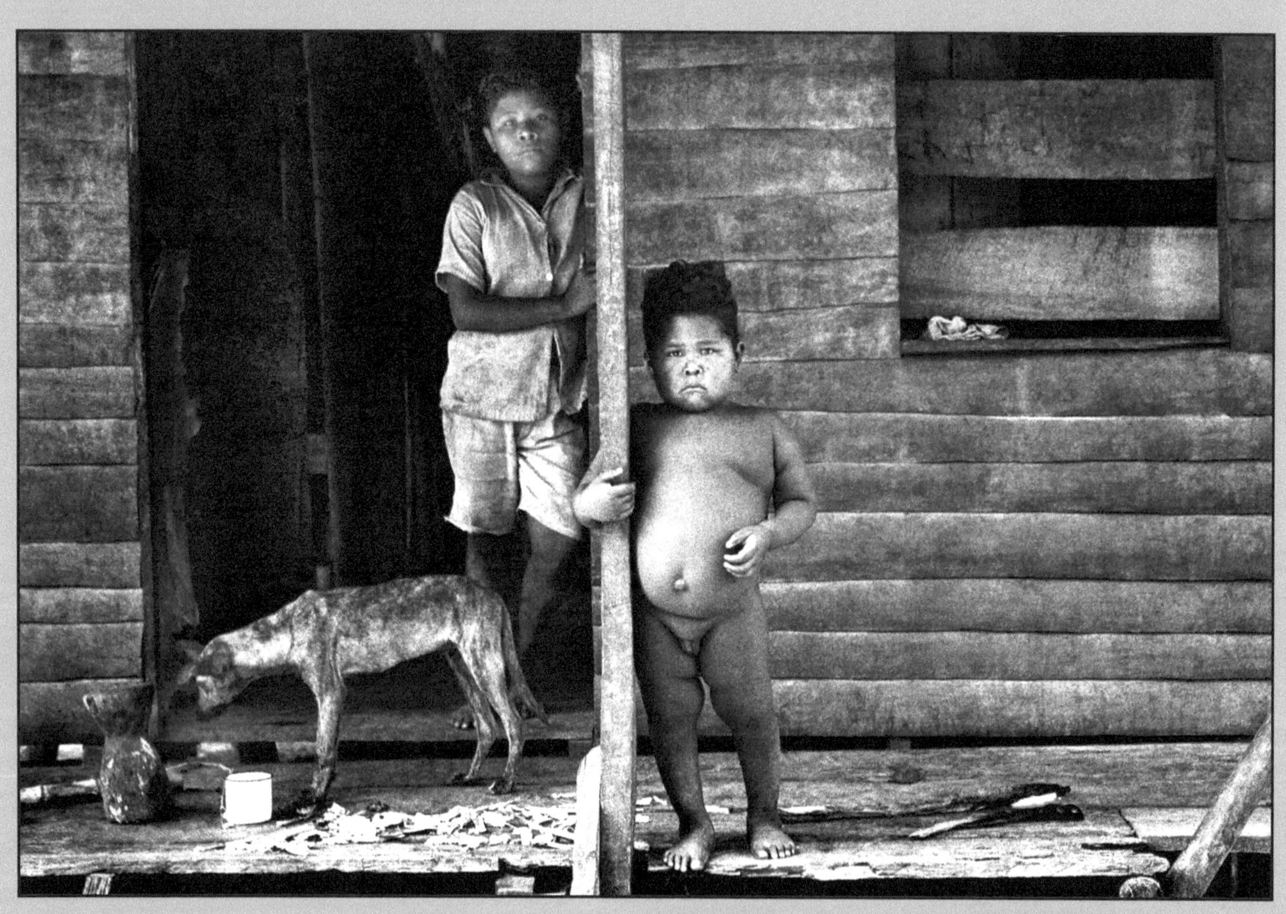

Gracias a Dios Department, Honduras - Miskoto Indian house 1968

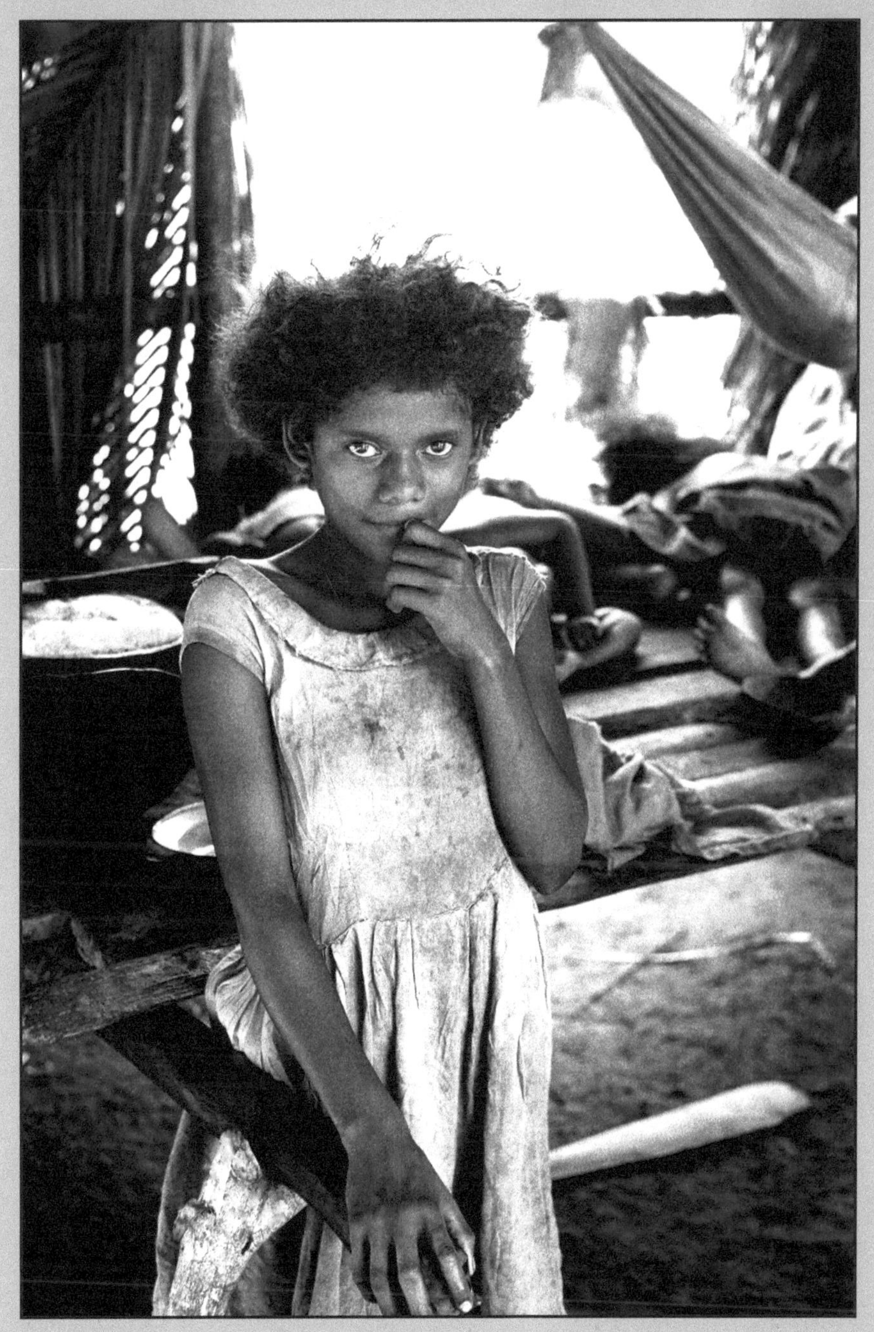

Gracias a Dios Department, Honduras - Miskoto Indian Girl 1968

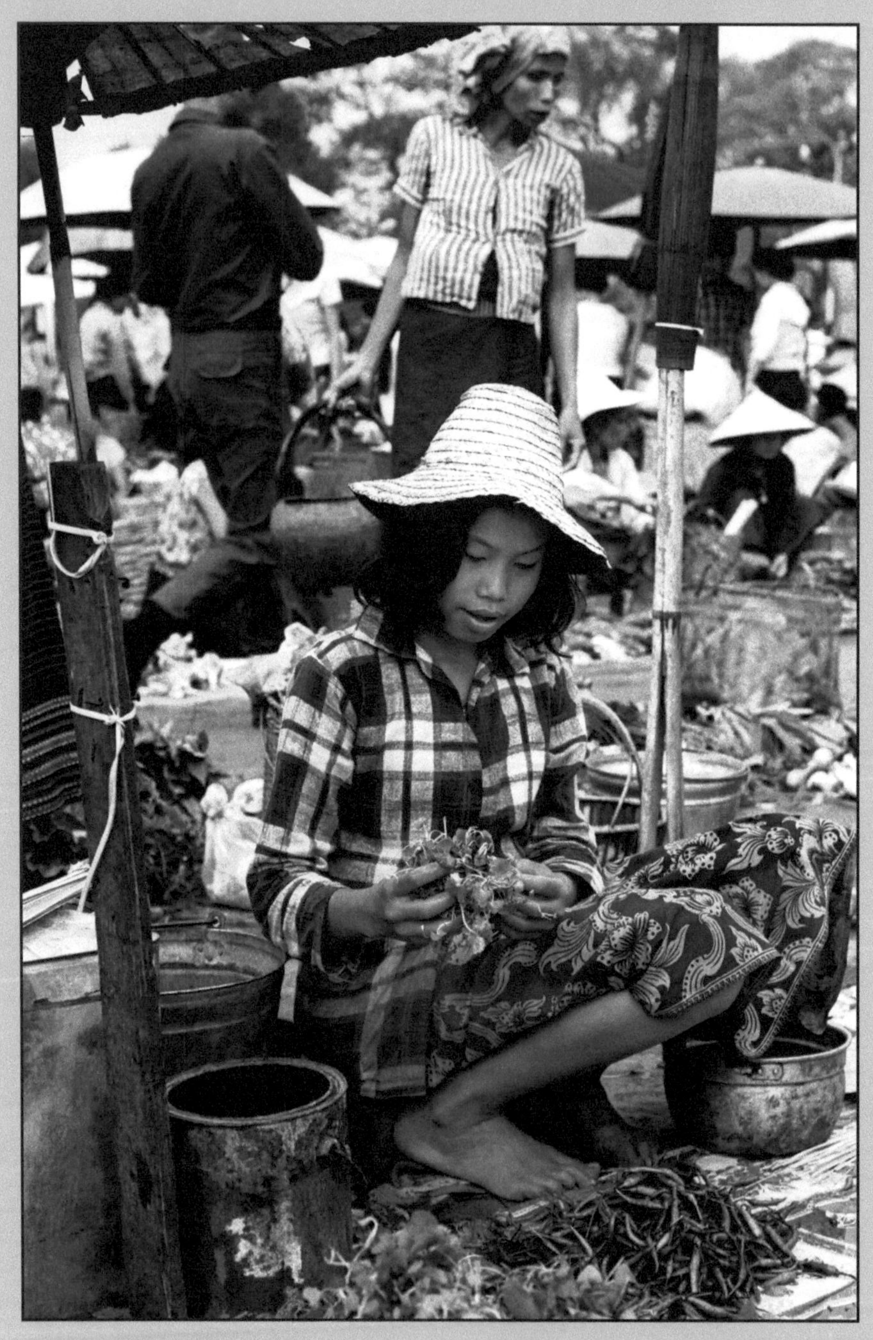

Vientiene, Laos – Central Market 1967

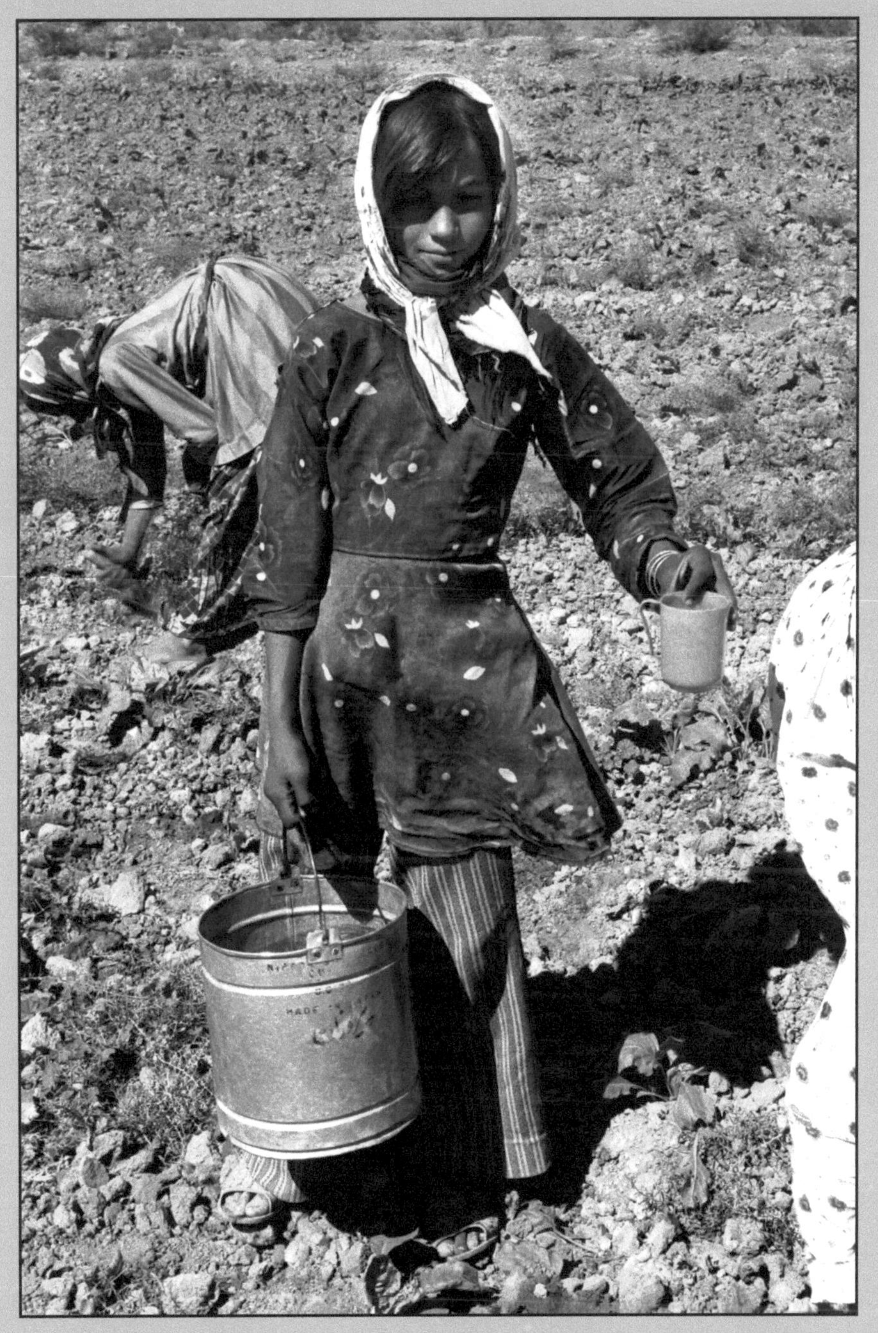

Khuzestan Province, Iran - Girl carrying water to field workers 1975

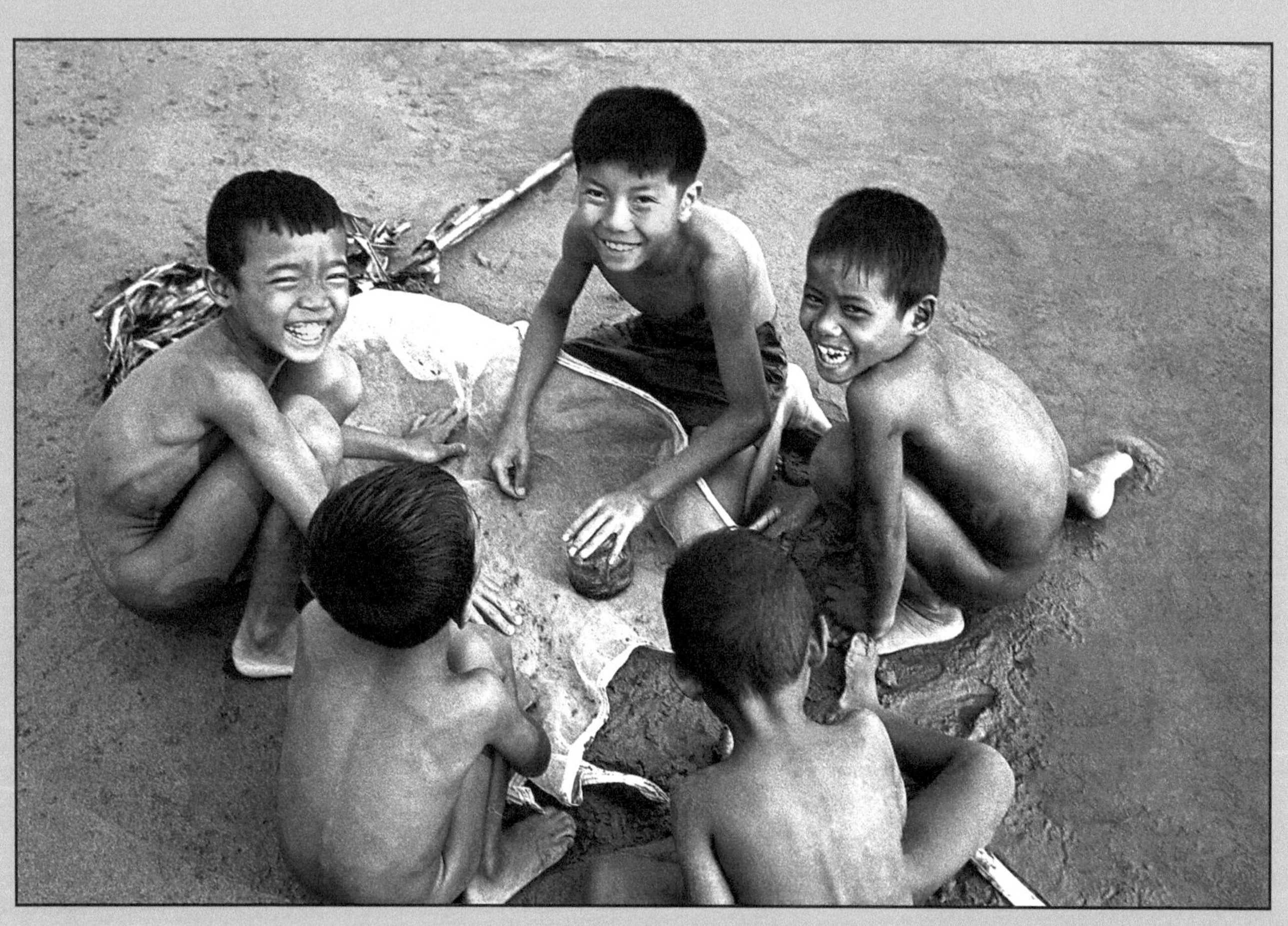

Vientiene, Laos - Boys at edge of the Mekong River 1967

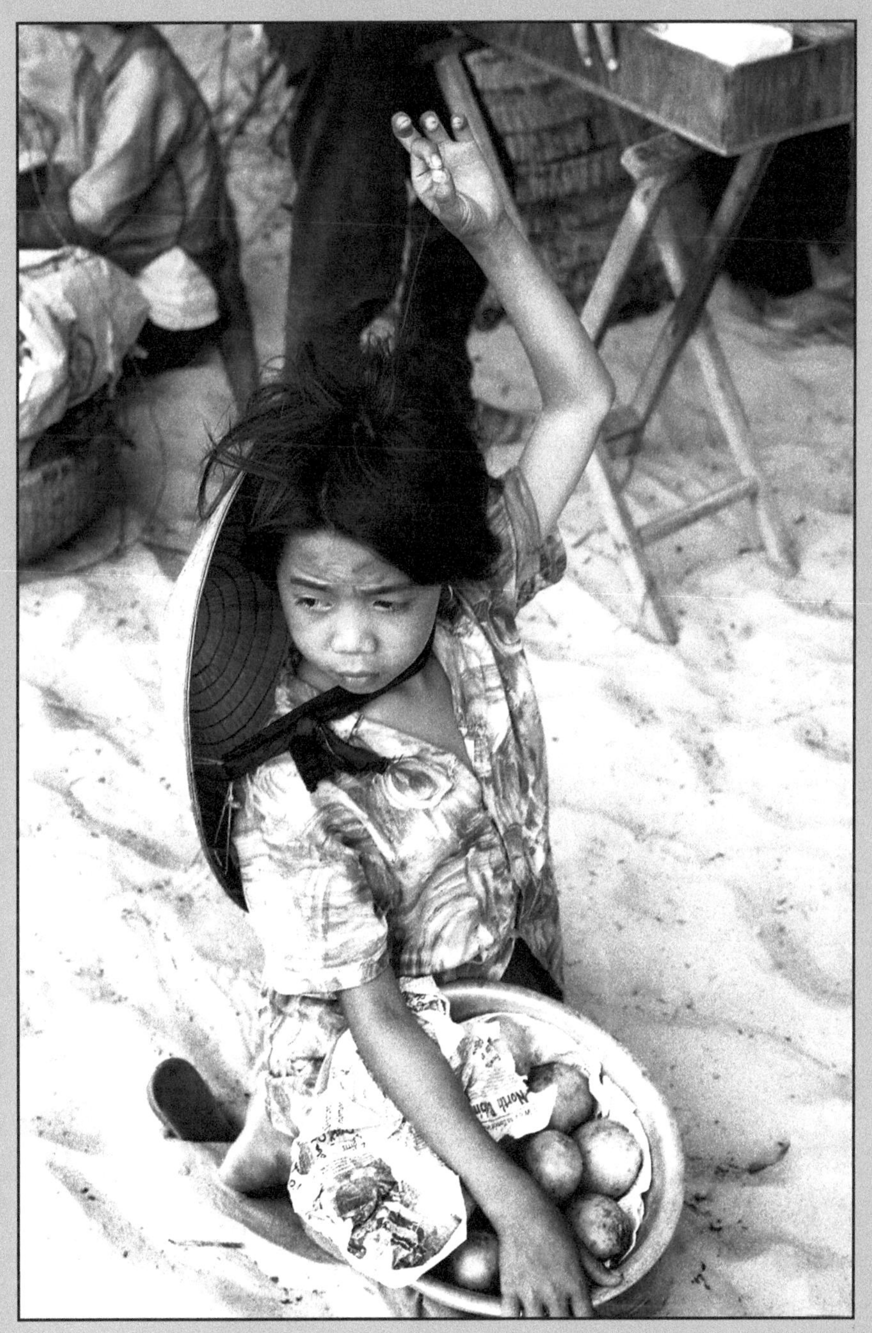

Nha Trang, Vietnam - Girl selling potatoes 1967

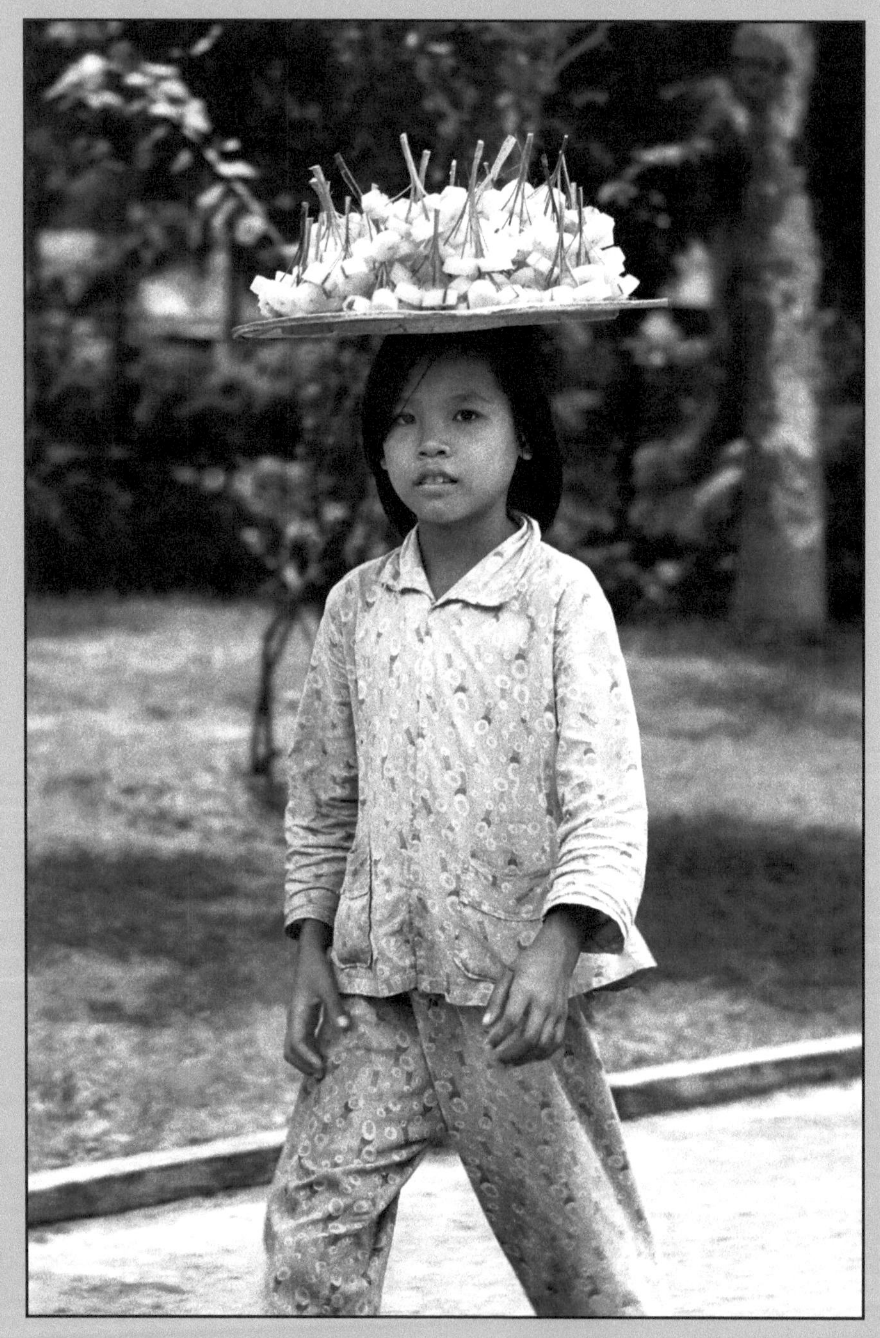

Saigon, Vietnam - Sugar cane vendor at Saigon Zoo 1966

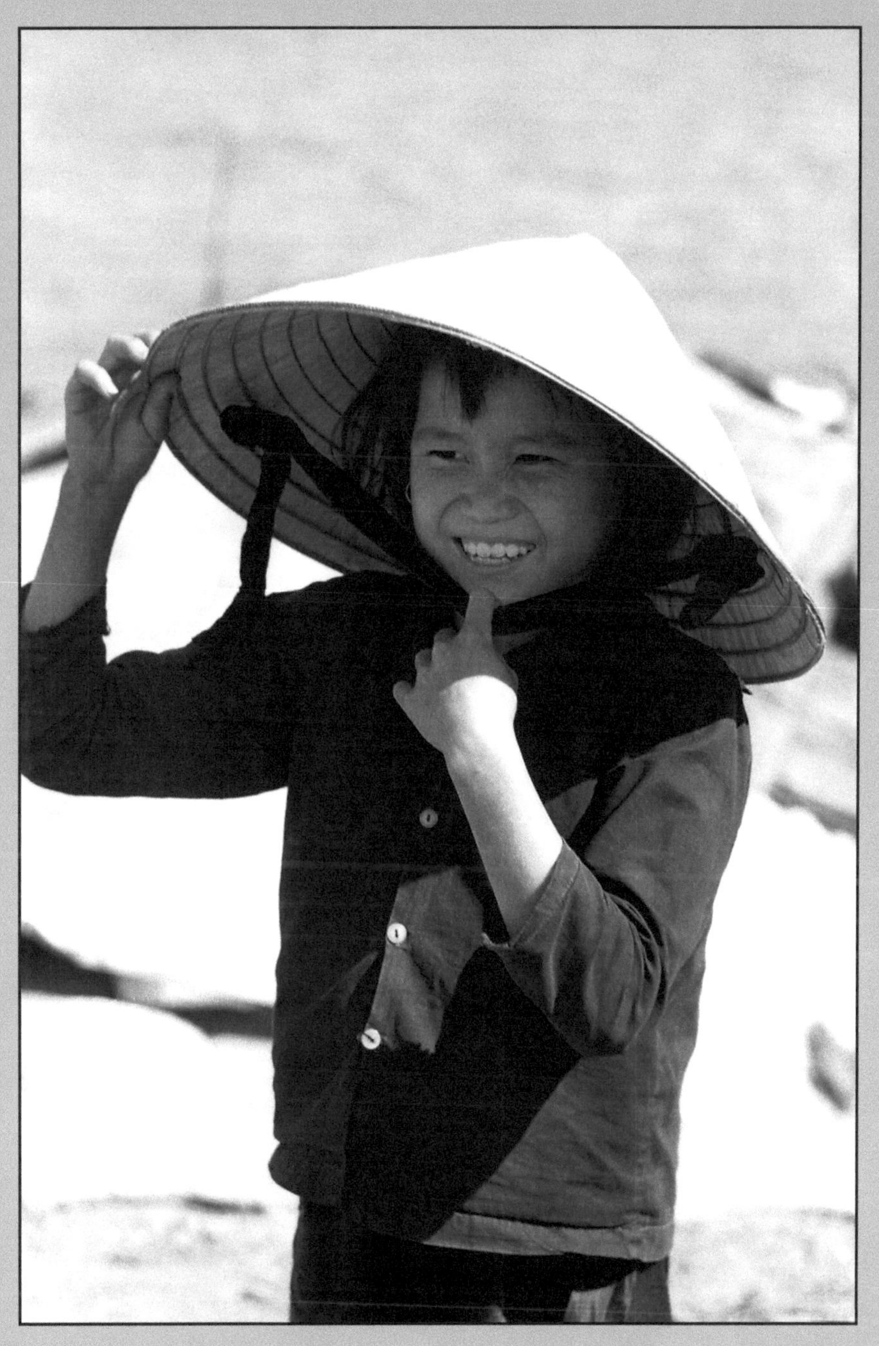

Da Nang, Vietnam - Young girl near the harbor 1966

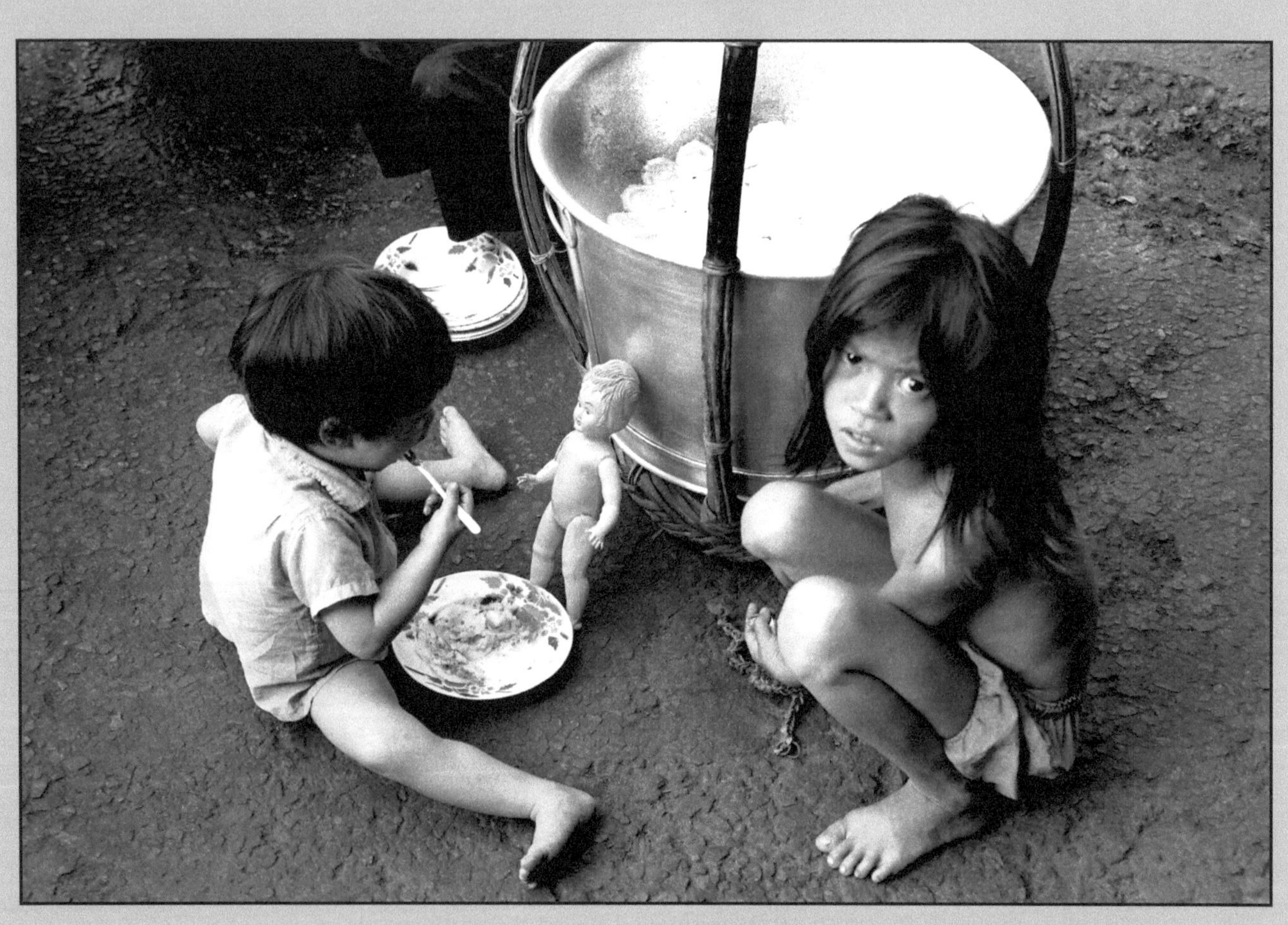

Saigon, Vietnam - Central Market 1966

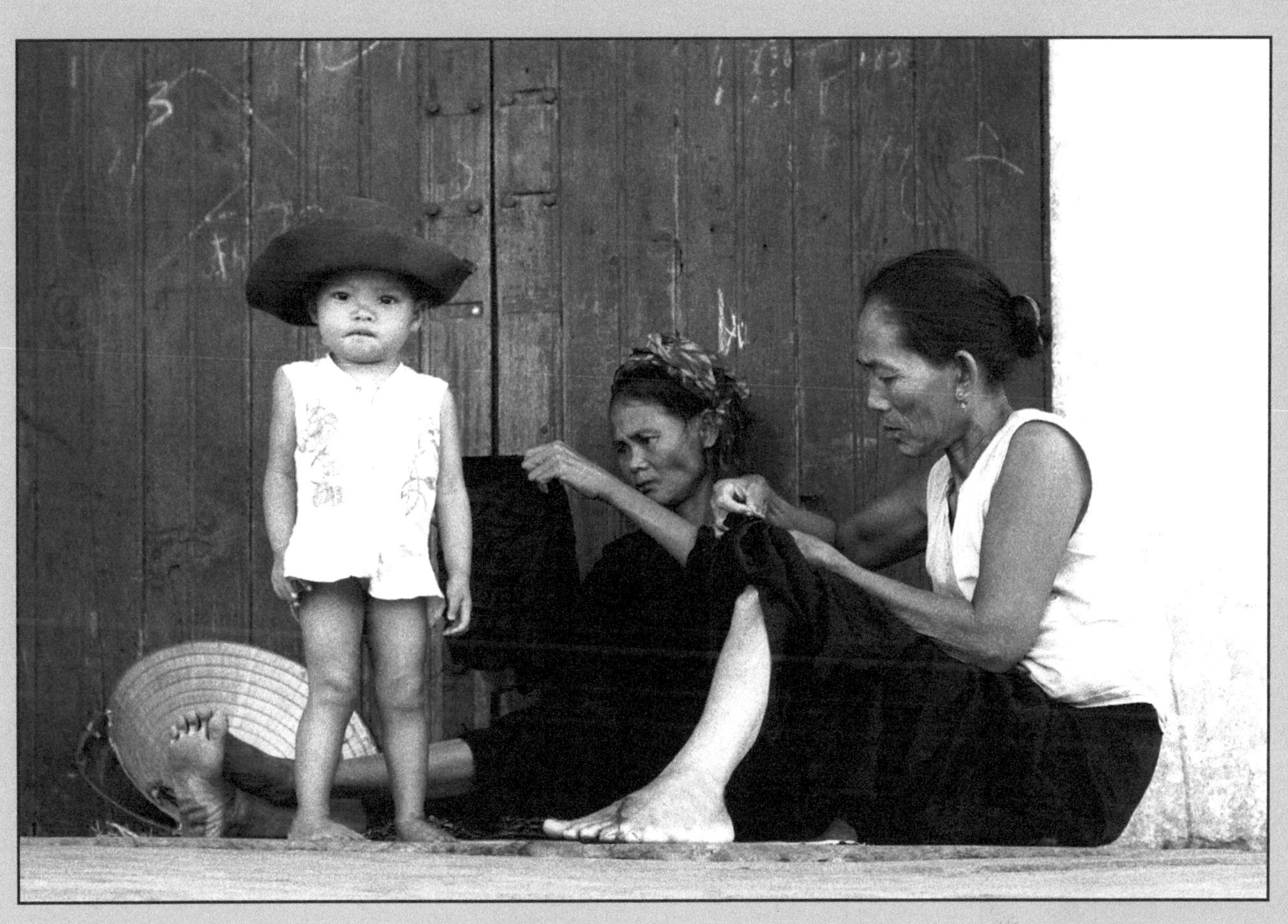

Da Nang, Vietnam - Street Scene along waterfront 1967

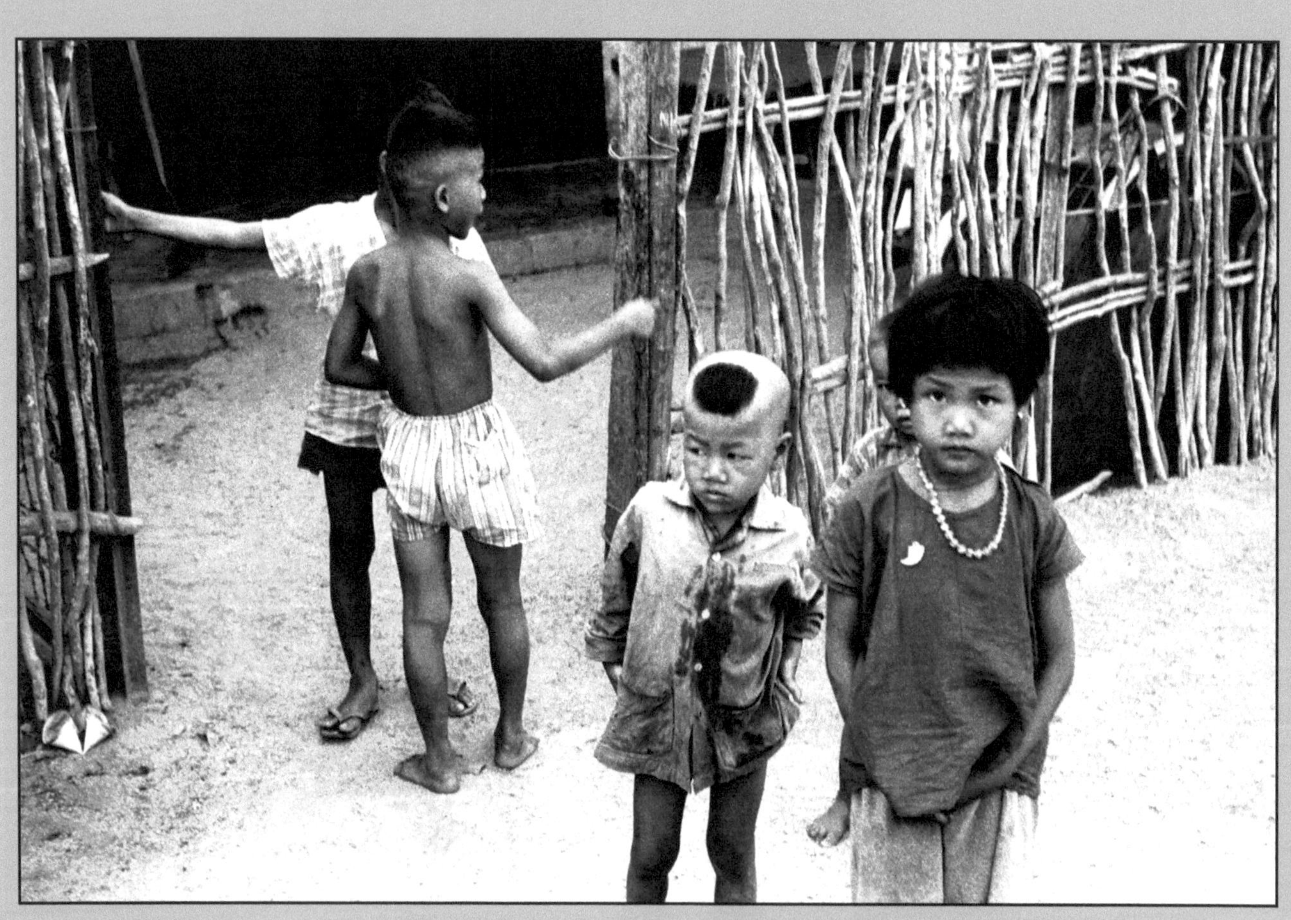

Nha Trang, Vietnam - Street Scene 1967

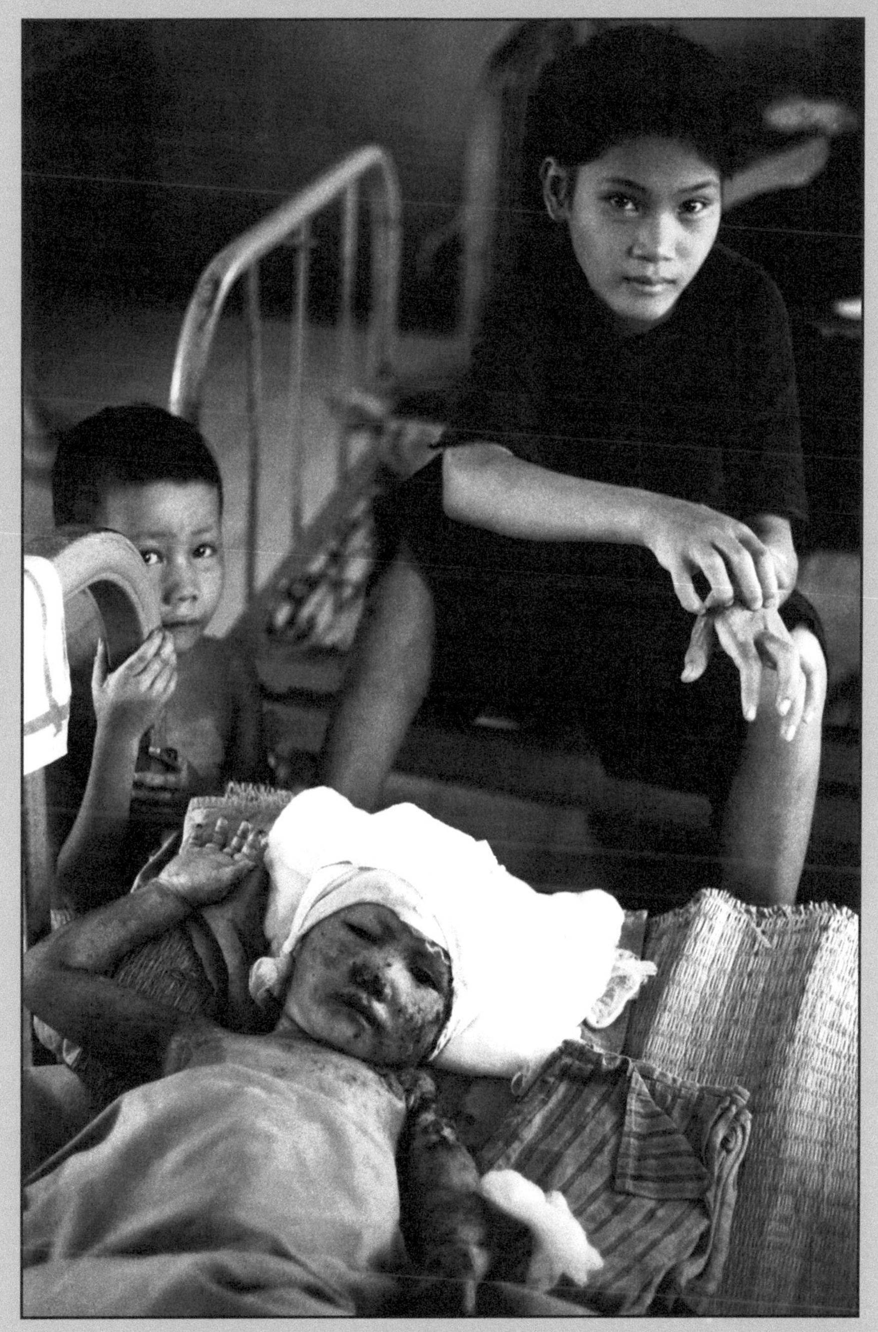

Da Nang, Vietnam - Burn ward at Da Nang Children's Hospital 1967

Photographer Bio

BOOKS: *REJOICE WHEN YOU DIE - The New Orleans Jazz Funerals (LSU Press 1998).*
DUET - Poet & Photographer - Elizabeth Burk & Leo Touchet (Yellow Flag Press 2018)
PEOPLE AMONG US - Photography by Leo Touchet (Photo Circle Press 2018)
AT THE RACES - Photography by Leo Touchet (Photo Circle Press 2018)
FLOWERS - In Black & White (Photo Circle Press 2018)
CHASING SHADOWS - Desert Sand Dunes (Photo Circle Press 2019)

COLLECTIONS: Sir Elton John Photography Collection, New Orelans Museum of Art, Houston Museum of Fine Arts, Bibliotheque National (France), Everson Museum of Art, Schomburg Center (New York Public Library), Chase Manhattan Collection, U.S. National Park Service.

PUBLICATIONS: Life Magazine, Time Magazine, Time Life Books, National Geographic Books, Newsweek Magazine, Fortune Magazine, Natural History Magazine, New York Times, Washington Post, Boston Globe, Oxford American Magazine, Southern Quarterly, Southern Living Magazine, America Illustrated (USIA), Der Stern (Germany), Panorama (Italy), Popular Photography.

EXHIBITIONS: Acadiana Center for the Arts, Arizona State University, Arkansas Art Center, Brooks Memorial (Memphis), Columbus Musuem (Georgia), Everson Museum (Syracuse), Fotofest '92 (Houston), Hofstra University (New York), Louisiana State University, Miami Art Center, Mint Museum (North Carolina), Mississippi Southern University, New Orleans Public Library, Oklahoma Art Center, Public Theater (New York City), Royal Ontario Museum (Toronto), University of Houston, University of Oklahoma, University of Texas.

GROUP EXHIBITIONS:
*REGARDS et MEMOIRES - ARLES 2008 - 39*th Annual Arles, France Photo Expo
(Four Exhibitions including Public Street Banners on the rue de la Roquette)
PHOTOGRAPHY USA 1976, United States Bicentennial Exhibition
(USIA exhibition circulated in the Soviet Union and East Europe).

Leo Touchet's Website: **www.leotouchet.com**

For Silver-Gelatin print sales: Contact Coco Conroy
coco@jacksonfineart.com
Jackson Fine Art Gallery in Atlanta, Georgia

Other Photo Books by
LEO TOUCHET

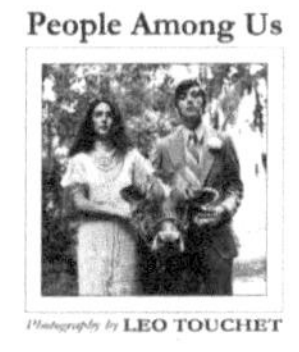

People Among Us - *Photography by Leo Touchet*

ISBN: 9781732443303 - 8.5 x 8.5 inches - 46 Pages - Paperback
Black & white photographs of people around the world.

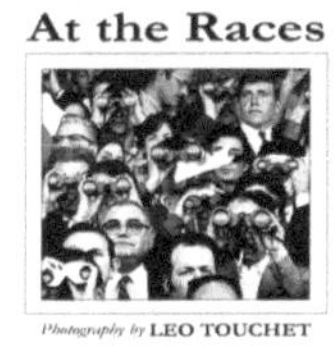

At The Races - *Photography by Leo Touchet*

ISBN: 9781732443310 - 8.5 x 8.5 inches - 42 Pages - Paperback
Black & white photographs people at horse races.

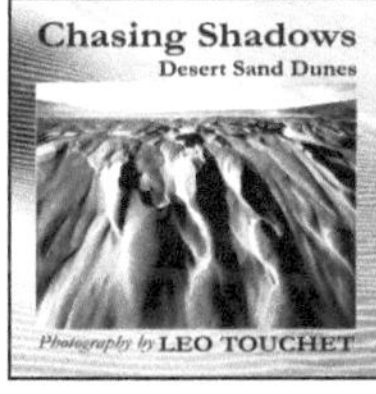

Chasing Shadows - *Desert Sand Dunes*

ISBN: 9781732443327 - 8.5 x 8.5 inches - 36 Pages - Paperback
Black & white photographs of desert sand dunes.

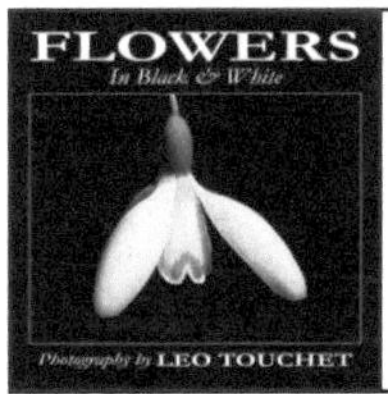

Flowers - *In Black & White*

ISBN: 9781732443334 - 8.5 x 8.5 inches - 36 Pages - Paperback
Black & white photographs of flowers.

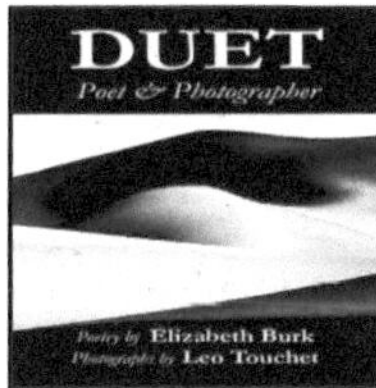

DUET - Poet & Photographer
Poet - **Elizabeth Burk** *Photographer* - **Leo Touchet**
ISBN: 9781387911103 - 8.5 x 8.5 inches - 60 Pages - Paperback
Published by Yellow Flag Press

These books are available from:

www.photocirclepress.com

www.ingramcontent.com/pod-product-compliance
Lightning Source LLC
LaVergne TN
LVHW070202110826
845147LV00002B/472

* 9 7 8 1 7 3 2 4 4 3 3 4 1 *